2020

Ingrid~

Whenever you open this book, we hope you will think back on this ver... special occasion when you celebrated your gra... and be reminded of how much we love you and how proud we are to have you as our granddaughter! Lots of love,

Grandma Byun
&
Grandpa Byun
xoxoxo

PRESENTED TO:

_____

PRESENTED BY:

_____

DATE:

_____

GOD'S
ROAD MAP
FOR GRADS

David Bordon and Tom Winters

WARNER
Faith ®

New York Boston Nashville

Concept: David Bordon and Tom Winters

Project Writing and Compilation: Molly Detweiler, Deborah Webb, Shanna
Gregor, and Betsy Williams in association with SnapdragonGroup[SM] Editorial
Services

Warner Faith
Time Warner Book Group
1271 Avenue of the Americas, New York, NY 10020
Visit our Web site at www.warnerfaith.com

Printed in the United States of America.
First Warner Books Edition: April 2006
10 9 8 7 6 5 4 3 2 1

ISBN: 0-446-57891-6

LCCN: 2005937104

INTRODUCTION

The road of life, as you know if you've been walking on it for very long, has many unmarked intersections and cross streets. Not only that, but it weaves up, down, and around through all types of landscapes and terrains. The journey provides moments of breathtaking beauty and others of abject fear. There are dark stretches, detours, and of course, there is the danger of getting lost. What's a traveler to do? Happily, God has provided a road map—the Bible—to help us avoid dangerous and time-consuming delays and to keep us on the path to our desired destination.

In *God's Road Map for Grads*, we have mined the Bible for wisdom and understanding that will be especially helpful for those of you who have reached a milestone in your education and are looking ahead to the next phase of your journey. We've included scriptures on certain topics of particular interest to graduates and laid them out in an A–Z format, so they will be simple for you to find and follow. We've also added to each topic an illustrative Bible story or practical devotional to help you on your way. Finally, we've provided heartfelt prayers and letters that express some of the thoughts and feelings God has given in His Word.

We hope you will find all you need as you travel the road of life and reach your next destination safely.

The Publishers

CONTENTS

Acceptance

Jesus said, "The one who comes to Me
I will certainly not cast out."
JOHN 6:37 NASB

Christ accepted you, so you should accept each other,
which will bring glory to God.
ROMANS 15:7 NCV

He made us accepted in the Beloved.
EPHESIANS 1:6 NKJV

Jesus said, "Whenever a village won't accept you or listen to you,
shake off the dust from your feet as you leave."
MARK 6:11 TLB

If you want favor with both God and man,
and a reputation for good judgment and common sense,
then trust the Lord completely.
PROVERBS 3:4–5 TLB

You bless the righteous, O LORD;
you cover them with favor as with a shield.
PSALM 5:12 NRSV

CONGRATULATIONS!
YOU'VE BEEN ACCEPTED

The young bride to be flashes her diamond and a bright
smile. She glows with the joy of acceptance. The newest
member of the company sighs with satisfaction as he looks at his
freshly printed business cards. He's part of the team and
feeling the power of acceptance! A new writer sees her first
article in print. She's now a published writer, experiencing the
excitement of acceptance.

Being accepted is one of the greatest feelings in the world.
We all long for it, but sometimes the price of being accepted
may be too high—the inner circle at work that assumes you will
wink at unethical office procedures—the group of up-and-
coming, young professionals who expect you to overlook their
drug and alcohol use—the boyfriend or girlfriend who pressures
you to have sex as a way to prove your love.

Finding acceptance without compromising your values may
mean that friends are harder to come by. Integrity-minded
individuals don't usually advertise their differences with the in
crowd. Those people are there if you look, though—almost
always staying just below the radar. Take the time to look for
them, and you may be happy to find true acceptance from those
who share your faith and values.

Remember, too, as you enter this next phase of your life,
there will be lonely times—times when you choose to take an
unpopular stand—times when you must forego the acceptance
of some in order to be at peace with yourself—times when you
alone understand the dream that's in your heart. At all times,
but especially during those times, God's love and acceptance
will see you through.

Adventure

God, who got you started in this spiritual adventure,
shares with us the life of his Son and our Master Jesus.
He will never give up on you. Never forget that.
1 CORINTHIANS 1:9 MSG

The people who know their God shall be strong,
and carry out great exploits.
DANIEL 11:32 NKJV

Your life is a journey you must travel with a deep consciousness
of God. It cost God plenty to get you out of that dead-end,
empty-headed life you grew up in. He paid with
Christ's sacred blood, you know.
1 PETER 1:17-19 MSG

[Hezekiah] held fast to GOD—never loosened his grip—and obeyed
to the letter everything GOD had commanded Moses. And GOD,
for his part, held fast to him through all his adventures.
2 KINGS 18:6-7 MSG

[The apostle Paul wrote,] I have no interest in giving you a chatty
account of my adventures, only the wondrously powerful and trans-
formingly present words and deeds of Christ in me that triggered a
believing response among the outsiders. In such ways I have trail-
blazed a preaching of the Message of Jesus.
ROMANS 15:18-19 MSG

LIVING THE ADVENTURE

Indiana Jones grabs the treasure and narrowly escapes the giant boulder rolling toward him. Spider-Man swings above the city to rescue Mary Jane. Brave Frodo faces the perils of Mordor. We love stories like these—even though they're fictional—because they draw out the hero and heroine in us all. They make us want to follow our destiny, just as God intended.

Of course, there have been many real-life adventurers, including those involved in the exciting exploits recorded in the Bible. Consider these: Abraham answered God's call to leave his comfortable life and make the epic journey to a land he had never even visited. Moses took his people out of bondage in Egypt and led them to and through the Red Sea—which parted at his command. Young David fought the giant Goliath—and won! Jesus' disciples lived for three years in the presence of healing and miracles. They witnessed their Master's death and resurrection. The New Testament apostle Paul survived shipwrecks, snakebites, imprisonment, and stoning. He preached to hostile crowds and appeared before kings. He even performed miracles by the power of God.

It's clear that God means for each of us to live adventurously for Him! And there is no greater time than now, as you graduate, to begin searching for the exciting and wonderful destiny He has prepared for you. With God as your guide, take every opportunity to fight the good fight of faith, boldly stand up for right and truth, and offer a helping hand to those in trouble. Don't hesitate another moment—your adventure is waiting!

Appearances

God does not judge by external appearance.

GALATIANS 2:6

What matters is not your outer appearance—
the styling of your hair, the jewelry you wear,
the cut of your clothes—but your inner disposition.

1 PETER 3:3 MSG

Jesus said, "Do not judge by appearances,
but judge with right judgment."

JOHN 7:24 NRSV

The LORD said to Samuel, ". . . The LORD doesn't make decisions
the way you do! People judge by outward appearance, but the LORD
looks at a person's thoughts and intentions."

1 SAMUEL 16:7 NLT

Jesus said, "If you decide for God, living a life of God-worship, it
follows that you don't fuss about what's on the table at mealtimes or
whether the clothes in your closet are in fashion. There is far more
to your life than the food you put in your stomach, more to your
outer appearance than the clothes you hang on your body."

MATTHEW 6:25 MSG

Charm is deceptive, and beauty is fleeting.

PROVERBS 31:30

Heavenly Father:

Sometimes I don't think that people see the real me. They only look at my outward appearance and form an opinion that isn't even accurate. It hurts when they write me off and don't take time to know me like You do.

I might not be the picture of perfection according to society's standards, but I'm so thankful that You know my heart and love me just as I am. What a relief it is that I never have to fake it with You.

I do want You to help me look my very best; but even more than that, I ask You to bring quality people into my life who will love me for who I am, who You made me. And help me to look past the outward appearance of others and see the real person inside, just as You do.

Amen.

THE HEART OF
A SHEPHERD BOY

You really want that job at the advertising agency, and now that you have your diploma in hand, you think you have a shot at it. But when you arrive for your interview and check out a few of the company's associates, your confidence wavers. They are all tall and slender, well dressed, and great looking. The receptionist looks like some kind of supermodel. Then you catch a glimpse of yourself in a mirror—and your confidence plummets all the way to the basement.

The great King David probably felt the same way when he was a young man. He had to tend sheep while his older, taller, more handsome brothers went off to battle, helped their father with important matters, and commanded the respect of others in the community.

But one day something remarkable happened. A prophet came calling. He said God had sent him to that very home to anoint the next king of Israel. In this case, the employer was God, and He was more interested in David's heart than his looks. His much better looking brothers were all passed over, and David was called in from the field.

You may not be a head-turner like Liv Tyler or Orlando Bloom, but the good news is that God isn't concerned with your outward appearance. There's nothing wrong with looking good, but God picked David to be king of a nation on the basis of his heart attitude. The Lord is searching for the same qualifications today. He has a great plan for your life, no matter how you rate in the looks department.

My Precious Child:

You were created to live from the inside out. Your spirit—the real you—springs forth from your heart. Your outward appearance is merely a reflection of the beauty within. I see you for who you are, and I know the great potential that I've placed in you. Never be afraid to let people see your heart. Those who look closely enough will see what I see and will be blessed by your special gifts.

Yes, I know your heart, but did you know that I want you to know Mine? Follow hard after Me as David did, and as you grow in your relationship with Me, you'll begin to reflect My image and realize your full potential—the you that I already see.

Your loving Father

Being Real

What good would it do to get everything you want and lose you,
the real you? What could you ever trade your soul for?

MARK 8:36-37 MSG

GOD, you are our Father.
We're the clay and you're our potter:
All of us are what you made us.

ISAIAH 64:8 MSG

The fear of human opinion disables;
trusting in GOD protects you from that.

PROVERBS 29:25 MSG

If the ear says, "I am not part of the body because I am only an ear
and not an eye," would that make it any less a part of the body?
Suppose the whole body were an eye—then how would you hear?
Or if your whole body were just one big ear, how could you smell
anything? But God made our bodies with many parts, and he has
put each part just where he wants it.

1 CORINTHIANS 12:16-18 NLT

The Lord is God! He made us—we are his people,
the sheep of his pasture.

PSALM 100:3 TLB

THE REAL THING

Cubic zirconia or diamond? Faux fur or real mink? Store-brand cola or Coke? Sometimes it's difficult to separate the real thing from the imitation. That's true about people, too. Many live their lives as mere copies of those around them. Rather than take the risk of exposing the true person inside, they project an image they consider acceptable because they fear ridicule or rejection. But how sad it is to think that the world may never see the real people God created them to be. That's why it's important to ask, how about you—are you real?

God made each of us with our own unique talents, skills, personality, and purpose. There is no one exactly like you. No one who can bring to the table the same combination of characteristics that you bring. Everyone loses when you refuse to let your true colors show.

Being real takes courage—especially since graduation may have separated you from your circle of safe friends and family. But don't let that stop you. Express yourself. Follow your bents. Identify those things that have real meaning for your life. Most of all, don't worry about what other people think about you. Some will like you no matter what you say and do. Others will push you away regardless of how strenuously you try to imitate their thoughts and actions.

This life is not a dress rehearsal. It's all you have—your chance to share with the world what you've been given. So don't be an imitation. God made you the real thing—and real is good.

Belonging

This is what the LORD says . . .
"Fear not, for I have redeemed you;
I have summoned you by name; you are mine."

ISAIAH 43:1

Praise be to the God and Father of our Lord Jesus Christ, who chose us in him before the creation of the world to be holy and blameless in his sight. In love he predestined us to be adopted as his sons through Jesus Christ, in accordance with his pleasure and will.

EPHESIANS 1:3-5

You belong to Christ; and Christ belongs to God.

1 CORINTHIANS 3:23 NASB

You are all one in Christ Jesus. And if you belong to Christ, then you are Abraham's offspring, heirs according to promise.

GALATIANS 3:28-29 NASB

In Christ we are all one body. Each one is a part of that body, and each part belongs to all the other parts.

ROMANS 12:5 NCV

LONGING TO BELONG

Belonging is one of our deepest needs. When we know that we belong, we feel free to be ourselves, to learn, and to grow. That's why new graduates often feel that their sense of belonging has been challenged as close friends go their separate ways and familiar surroundings are replaced by the unfamiliar.

You can be certain of this, however. No matter how your life's circumstances change, God's love for you, His concern and care, His desire for your success and well-being do not change. He makes it abundantly clear that He always belongs at your side and you always belong in His heart.

The Bible goes to great lengths to confirm this wonderful truth. Within its pages, you will find that God calls you His child, His son or daughter, His fellow worker, His ambassador, His shining star. He even calls you His jewel. He has promised that nothing in this world will ever be able to separate you from His love—nothing!

So no matter where life takes you as you begin this new chapter in your journey, remember that God has said you will always be part of His family. And because He loves you so much, He will help you find the human belonging you desire as well. New friends will make their way into your heart and you into theirs. God will lead you to places where your personality will shine and others will share your interests. You can count on that.

Change

The LORD says,
"Do not remember the former things,
Nor consider the things of old.
Behold, I will do a new thing,
Now it shall spring forth;
Shall you not know it?
I will even make a road in the wilderness
And rivers in the desert."

ISAIAH 43:18-19 NKJV

Moses said, "The LORD himself will go before you.
He will be with you; he will not leave you or forget you.
Don't be afraid and don't worry."

DEUTERONOMY 31:8 NCV

God said,
"I'll go ahead of you,
clearing and paving the road."

ISAIAH 45:2 MSG

I am the LORD, I change not.

MALACHI 3:6 KJV

Heavenly Father:

I made it—I have achieved my goal and graduated! But now I realize a lot of change is about to take place. I find myself excited and afraid at the same time.

Father, take me by the hand and walk with me through this new chapter in my life. Fill me with Your peace, and help me flow with the necessary adjustments I will have to make. Give me courage to let go of those things I need to leave behind, and help me embrace my future with my whole heart.

In the midst of this transition time, I'm so thankful that You are my Rock, the one constant I can always rely upon. Help me to keep my ultimate focus on You so that no matter what changes take place, I'll never lose sight of Your face.

Amen.

THE ROAD YET UNTRAVELED

Here you are a graduate—life stretching out before you like a long, untraveled road. A broad spectrum of colorful emotions are probably bubbling up from deep inside you—excitement, confusion, nervousness. You may even feel a little fearful of the unknown. One thing you can be sure of, though—practically nothing will remain the same. Friends will change. Routines will change. You may relocate to another city or get your own apartment. And most significant of all, you will begin living by a whole new set of rules.

One thing will stay the same, however—that's God. You may no longer be a "kid," but you'll always be God's child. Wherever life takes you, God will still be where He has always been—right with you, loving you, guiding you, and protecting you. He has promised that a bright future lies ahead, and He will be there to help you adjust to the changes.

The great patriarch Abraham faced such a situation in his life also. God asked him to leave behind all that was familiar and move his family to a faraway land. All he took with him were his faith and God's promise that there were great things ahead.

The coming changes in your life may not be as all-encompassing as they were in Abraham's life, but the principle remains the same. God stands with you as you face the future. Place your hand in His strong, assuring hand, and put your faith in His never-failing promises. Your future is bright. Embrace it!

My Precious Child:

No matter where you go on your journey, I will always be there and will never leave your side. I am constantly loving you, guiding you, and protecting you, and I will never let you down.

I know change can be scary, but keep in mind that the changes I bring about are always good. They stretch you and cause you to grow, giving you a larger capacity to embrace each adventure I have planned for you. Your future is bright; there is nothing to fear.

Together, My child, you and I can do anything, and I am cheering you on as you take each step. It is with great joy that I watch you becoming the person I created you to be.

Your loving Father

Church

Let us not give up meeting together, as some are in the habit of doing, but let us encourage one another—and all the more as you see the Day approaching.

HEBREWS 10:25

Jesus said, "Where two or three are gathered in my name, there am I in the midst of them."

MATTHEW 18:20 RSV

The church everywhere . . . had a time of peace and became stronger. Respecting the Lord by the way they lived, and being encouraged by the Holy Spirit, the group of believers continued to grow.

ACTS 9:31 NCV

Each one should use whatever gift he has received to serve others, faithfully administering God's grace in its various forms. If anyone speaks, he should do it as one speaking the very words of God. If anyone serves, he should do it with the strength God provides, so that in all things God may be praised through Jesus Christ.

1 PETER 4:10-11

The churches became stronger in the faith and grew larger every day.

ACTS 16:5 NCV

IS IT REALLY THAT IMPORTANT?

What is your first thought when someone mentions church? Do you think of Sunday mornings and getting dressed up? Or is church a place you have visited only on holidays? Maybe church doesn't really have any meaning to you because you've never attended. Now that you've graduated and are on your own, you have a choice about where, when, and even if, you will go to church. Maybe you're wondering if it is really that important. Why should church be a part of your already busy schedule?

First of all, God longs for you to be with Him in His house. While you can be with God wherever you are, there is something special about gathering with other people to meet with Him together. When we do, we encourage each other, show the world the power of God's love, and bring joy to God in the process.

While attending church is pleasing to God, being part of a church is also one of the ways that God blesses you. He wants to use your church to bring you deep friendships with other people who love Him. He wants to help you learn what it really means to follow Him through the messages you hear or Bible studies you attend. And He also uses your local church to provide you with opportunities to exercise the gifts and talents He has given you.

So take the time to visit a few churches. Ask God to guide you to the one that is just right for you. When you find a group of believers to belong to, you'll find that the word "church" has a whole new and wonderful meaning for your life.

Confidence

I am confident of this very thing, that He who began a good work
in you will perfect it until the day of Christ Jesus.
PHILIPPIANS 1:6 NASB

You are my hope;
O LORD GOD, You are my confidence from my youth.
PSALM 71:5 NASB

The Fear-of-GOD builds up confidence.
PROVERBS 14:26 MSG

The LORD will be your confidence
and will keep your foot from being snared.
PROVERBS 3:26

The effect of righteousness will be quietness and
confidence forever.
ISAIAH 32:17

As they observed the confidence of Peter and John, . . . they were
amazed, and began to recognize them as having been with Jesus.
ACTS 4:13 NASB

BUILDING CONFIDENCE

Whom do you most admire? Whom do you look up to as a role model for your own life? What qualities do these individuals possess that inspire you? While there are probably a whole list of great attributes you could name, one of them is probably confidence. The most successful people are usually the most confident. They know what their goals are, and they work toward them with the expectation that they will succeed. This confidence is contagious, too—it inspires confidence in others.

Now that you're a graduate, you're heading into a new chapter of your life. You're facing a lot of unknowns, and it is sometimes difficult to have that confidence you so admire. If you're feeling unsure and frustrated by your own lack of confidence, don't despair! Even the brightest and most successful people in our world were once new in their fields. No one is born with absolute confidence—it is something that is developed as a person grows and learns. Allow yourself some time to grow into your new roles, and celebrate each small victory as a step toward greater confidence in yourself and your abilities.

Another thing to remember is that God already believes in you! He created you with your own special set of positive attributes and talents, and He wants to help you develop them. So when you struggle with self-doubt, know that God is on your side, ready to help you grow and become confident in the gifts He's given you. He promises to help you become all you can be if you will only ask!

Conflict

Those who control their anger have great understanding;
those with a hasty temper will make mistakes.

PROVERBS 14:29 NLT

People with good sense restrain their anger.

PROVERBS 19:11 NLT

Stay away from foolish and stupid arguments,
because you know they grow into quarrels. And a servant of the
Lord must not quarrel but must be kind to everyone,
a good teacher, and patient. The Lord's servant must gently teach
those who disagree. Then maybe God will let them change their
minds so they can accept the truth.

2 TIMOTHY 2:23-25 NCV

Work at getting along with each other and with God.
Otherwise you'll never get so much as a glimpse of God.

HEBREWS 12:14 MSG

Pride only breeds quarrels,
but wisdom is found in those who take advice.

PROVERBS 13:10

Heavenly Father:

Conflict is so uncomfortable. You know the situation going on right now and how easily I could get sucked up into strife. Show me what part I am to play and how You want me to handle it. I don't want to react angrily and say things I will later regret, but I also don't want to just stick my head in the sand, hoping the problem will go away. If you want to use me to bring about positive change, I am willing.

First, help me keep my heart right so Your love can flow through me. Help me choose my words wisely so that they have a productive and healing effect on the situation. You know how to resolve this conflict so that everybody wins, so I ask You to help us do that.

Amen.

GOD'S CONFLICT-RESOLUTION PLAN

From arguing with a sibling over a toy when you're three to struggling with a coworker over an important project, conflict is a fact of life. Now, as a graduate, you're heading into a whole new world of bigger challenges and greater potential for conflict with others.

The bad news is that conflict isn't going to go away or get easier now that you're a full-fledged adult. But there is good news, too. The ultimate source of wisdom, the Bible, has a specific road map for dealing with conflict and solving it.

The first step to working out any dispute is to talk to the other person one-on-one. Talking behind someone's back only adds fuel to the conflict fire. Discussing the problem face-to-face will often put an end to conflict quickly. You may even make a good friend in the process.

Unfortunately, some people are harder to deal with than others. If you do your best to solve a problem face-to-face but end up getting nowhere, God's advice is to bring another person along with you and try again. Make sure that this third person is someone who can be impartial and hear both sides.

If this still doesn't help you solve the problem, then it is time to enlist the help of professionals. Ask your pastor, a counselor, or if it is work-related, your human resources director to get involved. The important thing is to keep working toward a solution. When you follow God's guidelines, you won't avoid conflicts entirely, but through His wisdom, you can solve them more quickly and in a way that will bring His peace to the situation.

My Precious Child:

I knew you would face conflict, and I've prepared for it. My Word offers excellent advice. I wrote it with you in mind. It takes work on your part, but it is well worth it in the end.

When you go to the person with whom there is a problem, it opens the door of communication. If you are unable to resolve the issue, bring in a mediator who will give both sides an opportunity to be heard. Then really listen and put yourself in the other person's position.

Remember, in some ways you're both on the same side. Find the points of agreement and build upon them. Seek a solution that benefits everyone involved. Peace is the final outcome of a well orchestrated conflict, and I will help you get there.

Your loving Father

Contentment

I have learned the secret of contentment in every situation,
whether it be a full stomach or hunger, plenty or want;
for I can do everything God asks me to with the help of Christ
who gives me the strength and power.

PHILIPPIANS 4:12-13 TLB

Don't push your way to the front;
don't sweet-talk your way to the top. Put yourself aside,
and help others get ahead.

PHILIPPIANS 2:3 MSG

Keep your lives free from the love of money and
be content with what you have, because God has said,
"Never will I leave you; never will I forsake you."

HEBREWS 13:5

There is great gain in godliness combined with contentment;
for we brought nothing into the world, so that we can take nothing
out of it; but if we have food and clothing,
we will be content with these.

1 TIMOTHY 6:6-8 NRSV

THE POSSESSIONS PERSPECTIVE

You're always hearing that it is important to be content with what you have and that material possessions don't equal happiness. Yet every commercial says to get more nice "stuff" and you'll be admired and happy. As you embark on a new career and begin earning your own way, how will you handle your desire for material things? How do you avoid materialism and find true contentment?

Gaining the right perspective on what is really important in life can help. Here are some wise words from God's viewpoint:

- Money and possessions can disappear in an instant. God, on the other hand, will always be there for you. He will always provide what you need.

- Gaining a reputation as a kind and generous person is worth far more than money. You can't buy a good name for yourself.

- Having a lot of stuff leads to stress. It takes a lot of effort to take care of it all.

- The lust for more requires you to work harder and results in not having time to enjoy what you already have.

- Having money and nice things isn't wrong. When God blesses you with abundance, though, that is your chance to bless others—which brings you more blessing in return.

- If you truly want to love God, then you can't love money. Jesus said that you have to pick one or the other. So, which will you pick? The God of the universe who loves you eternally or the stuff of this world that will eventually end up in the landfill?

Look at possessions and money with God's perspective, and you'll be satisfied with lasting contentment.

Courage

Be strong and courageous. Do not be afraid or terrified
because of them, for the LORD your God goes with you;
he will never leave you nor forsake you.

DEUTERONOMY 31:6

Be strong in the Lord and in the power of His might.
Put on the whole armor of God, that you may be able to stand
against the wiles of the devil.

EPHESIANS 6:10-11 NKJV

Keep alert, stand firm in your faith, be courageous, be strong.

1 CORINTHIANS 16:13 NRSV

Don't lose your courage or be afraid. Don't panic or be frightened,
because the LORD your God goes with you, to fight for you
against your enemies and to save you.

DEUTERONOMY 20:3-4 NCV

LORD, you are my shield,
my wonderful God who gives me courage.

PSALM 3:3 NCV

Do not lose the courage you had in the past, which has a great
reward. You must hold on, so you can do what God wants and
receive what he has promised.

HEBREWS 10:35-36 NCV

EACH SMALL STEP

When you hear the word *courage*, what comes to mind? Perhaps you think about the firefighters who dashed into the crumbling World Trade Center on September 11 or the brave young soldiers fighting in Iraq and Afghanistan. Maybe you think about someone you know personally—a relative who is facing cancer with an incredibly positive attitude or a friend who teaches in an inner-city school in the midst of daily violence.

All around us are people who show us what it means to be courageous. But what about you? Do you think of yourself as courageous? Maybe you're not a rescue worker or a cancer survivor, but every day, in a thousand small ways, you, too, are being courageous. As a graduate, you are facing a lot of change and uncertainty; and with the unknown comes fear. But as you push past your fear and take steps of faith, you are showing and building courage.

When you send out your résumé for that new job, you're being courageous. When you make an effort to meet your new neighbor, you're being courageous. When you get up on Sunday morning and walk into a new church for the first time, you're being courageous. And with each seemingly small step, you're building courage for even bigger challenges that will come in the future.

Over and over in the Bible, God says, "Don't be afraid" and "Be courageous." So as you begin this new chapter of your life, remember that each small, brave step you take is important—and pleasing to your Father. And when you ask Him for courage to continue facing the challenges of each new day, He will be faithful to provide.

Dating

I am a companion of all those who fear You,
And of those who keep Your precepts.

PSALM 119:63 NASB

Whoever walks with the wise becomes wise,
but the companion of fools suffers harm.

PROVERBS 13:20 NRSV

You are not the same as those who do not believe.
So do not join yourselves to them. Good and bad do not belong
together. Light and darkness cannot share together. . . .
What can a believer have together with a nonbeliever?

2 CORINTHIANS 6:14-15 NCV

Two are better than one because they have a good return for their
labor. For if either of them falls, the one will lift up his companion.

ECCLESIASTES 4:9-10 NASB

Practice God's law—get a reputation for wisdom;
hang out with a loose crowd—embarrass your family.

PROVERBS 28:7 MSG

Heavenly Father:

Dating can be so frustrating. Sometimes I find myself pretending to be someone I'm not, just to impress others. But I don't want to build a future on lies. Help me to be comfortable with who You made me to be.

I also need Your help not to compromise my values or the plan You have for my life. Help me to keep my emotions in check and to keep the big picture in mind. I don't want to miss out on any of the good things You have for me.

Relationships play such a large role in life, and I ask You to orchestrate the ones You have for me, helping me recognize the place each person is to hold. And until I meet the person You've ordained for me to marry, help me remain patient and keep my eyes on You.

Amen.

TRIAL RUN

Dating was so simple when you were in school. You were surrounded by people your age every day, you shared many of the same interests and activities, and you attended many of the same social events. In other words, you had a built-in pool of candidates and a ready-made list of opportunities. All you had to do was find the match and muster the courage to ask.

Dating after graduation—that's altogether different. You must track down a candidate, determine whether you have any common interests, and be creative about what activities you want to engage in.

While they might not make it easier, here are three things to remember that might make dating more enjoyable:

1. Remember who you are. Be yourself. Don't work too hard at making a good impression. Authenticity is appealing. Place yourself in situations where you'll meet people with common values and interests. In other words, if you don't like fast cars, don't hang out at the drag races.

2. Remember what you want. Don't compromise your goals or values in order to be popular. People are drawn to individuals who know what they stand for and what they aspire to become.

3. Remember where you're headed. If you are pursuing a particular career path or intend to further your education, you need to stay focused on where it will lead you in life. You don't want to get attached to a cactus farmer if you hope to be a marine biologist.

Dating is not a game. It is more like a trial run for a lifetime relationship. Take it seriously.

My Precious Child:

View each person you date as a potential friend, and if nothing more serious develops, your life will still be richer for having known that individual. As you keep your relationship with Me your first priority, you will be wise and discerning in this area.

For any relationship to be successful, I must be the first common denominator. Steer clear of those who don't know Me.

I know that some say love is blind, but I want you to date with your eyes wide open. The only way to determine if you are compatible with another person is for you to be true to who you are and to get to know the real person you're dating.

Finally, keep all your relationships pure so that when you do meet the person I've planned for you to marry, you will be able to build your future on a strong foundation.

Your loving Father

Decisions

I am the LORD your God,
who teaches you what is best for you,
who directs you in the way you should go.

ISAIAH 48:17

People throw lots to make a decision,
but the answer comes from the LORD.

PROVERBS 16:33 NCV

I will instruct you and teach you in the way you should go;
I will counsel you and watch over you.

PSALM 32:8

Without counsel, plans go awry,
But in the multitude of counselors
they are established.

PROVERBS 15:22 NKJV

Jesus said, "Father, . . . not My will, but Yours, be done."

LUKE 22:42 NKJV

DECISIONS, DECISIONS

Decisions—now that you've graduated, you're facing what seems like a million big choices every day. After years of having many of your decisions made for you, the freedom to choose can be both exciting and terrifying. But while you're responsible for your own choices now, that doesn't mean you have to make them alone. God has provided you with a whole book of good advice on how to make the best decisions. Here are a few tips from the ultimate guidebook—the Bible:

- Get advice from people who have a proven track record of making good decisions in their own lives.
- Use the Bible as a guide. Will your decision please God? For example, is it based on pure motives and a desire to follow His purpose or is it based on your desire for money or status?
- How will your decision affect others? While you can't make all your choices based on what others want, it is always good to consider others as much as possible.
- Pray, pray again, and pray some more. God is the creator of wisdom, so when you talk to Him about your decisions, you are seeking guidance from the best source in the world!

Making decisions is never easy, especially ones that will affect the rest of your life. Just remember that you don't have to go it alone. God is ready and willing to guide you through His Word, prayer, and the advice of the wise people He has placed in your life. When you seek His wisdom, He will never fail to provide.

Discernment

If you want better insight and discernment, and are searching for
them as you would for lost money or hidden treasure, then wisdom
will be given you, and knowledge of God himself.

PROVERBS 2:3-5 TLB

I ask—ask the God of our Master, Jesus Christ, the God of glory—
to make you intelligent and discerning in knowing him personally,
your eyes focused and clear, so that you can see exactly
what it is he is calling you to do.

EPHESIANS 1:17-18 MSG

Those who are unspiritual do not receive
the gifts of God's Spirit, for they are foolishness to them,
and they are unable to understand them because they are spiritually
discerned. Those who are spiritual discern all things, and they are
themselves subject to no one else's scrutiny.

1 CORINTHIANS 2:14-15 NRSV

This is my prayer: that your love may abound more and more in
knowledge and depth of insight, so that you may be able to discern
what is best and may be pure and blameless until the day of Christ.

PHILIPPIANS 1:9-10

Do not be conformed to this world, but be transformed by the
renewing of your minds, so that you may discern what is the will of
God—what is good and acceptable and perfect.

ROMANS 12:2 NRSV

DREAMS AND DISCERNMENT

You could say that Solomon had just "graduated" too. He was probably about twenty-one when his father, David, died—and Solomon was promoted from prince to king. He knew that he needed help to be an effective leader for his people—the task was just too big to handle alone. And so, Solomon went to the ultimate source of guidance—God.

After a full day of intense worship and prayer, Solomon fell into a deep sleep. During the night, God spoke to Solomon in his dream. "Solomon, ask Me for whatever you want and I'll give it to you."

Wow! If God said that to you, what would you ask for? Solomon could have asked for anything in the world—money, peace for his kingdom, or even revenge on his enemies—but he didn't.

Instead Solomon admitted to the Lord that he was just a kid and that he didn't have the experience or knowledge he needed to be king, and so he asked for one simple thing—discernment. All Solomon truly wanted from God was to have wisdom and sound judgment. God was thrilled with Solomon's answer. He promised Solomon that he wouldn't just be discerning but that he would be the wisest man ever! And as a bonus, he would get riches and peace for his kingdom as well. (See I Kings 3:5-15.)

You may not be graduating into a new job as big as Solomon's, but you are facing new challenges that call for discernment. The same God who provided wisdom to Solomon wants to give you a discerning heart and sound judgment—all you have to do is ask.

Doubt

Lord, when doubts fill my mind, when my heart is in turmoil,
quiet me and give me renewed hope and cheer.

PSALM 94:19 TLB

Jesus said, "Anything is possible if a person believes." The father
instantly replied, "I do believe, but help me not to doubt!"

MARK 9:23-24 NLT

He has given us both his promise and his oath,
two things we can completely count on, for it is impossible
for God to tell a lie. Now all those who flee to him to save them
can take new courage when they hear such assurances from God;
now they can know without doubt that he will give them
the salvation he has promised them.

HEBREWS 6:18 TLB

Faith comes from hearing the message,
and the message is heard through the word of Christ.

ROMANS 10:17

Be merciful to those who doubt.

JUDE 1:22 TLB

Heavenly Father:

More than anyone, You know what I'm going through right now and the struggle taking place within me. As I meditate on Your promises, my faith is strong; I just know You will come through for me. At other times, however, it is as if the circumstances wash over me, flooding my soul with doubts that threaten to overtake me.

I see in Your Word that time after time, when Your servants clung to You and hoped against hope, You were faithful to Your promises. In fact, it seems that You delight in performing great miracles against all odds. But that is what makes You God and one of the reasons I love You so.

Help me to keep my focus on You and Your Word, so my doubts will be silenced until I see the answer come to pass.

Amen.

DEFEATING DOUBT

Do you have doubts—about yourself, about your relationships, or about God? If so, you're not alone. Even the biggest heroes of the Bible dealt with doubt:

- When God told Moses to go to Egypt and free His people, Moses doubted himself so much that he told God to find someone else for the job.
- In the book of Psalms, King David expresses his doubts about God when he sees people getting away with all kinds of evil while the people who are trying to follow God struggle.
- Joseph, Jesus' earthly father, doubted Mary's claim that she was pregnant with the Son of God and decided to call off their marriage.

During this time in your life, when you are leaving behind the familiar and graduating into a whole new life, doubts are bound to plague you. As you deal with your own areas of uncertainty, look at how God helped Moses, David, and Joseph move from a place of doubt into a new and deeper faith:

- God gave Moses the ability to perform miracles so that he could face Pharaoh.
- While David wrote about his doubts, he also wrote about the love and faithfulness God so clearly demonstrated to him when things were hard.
- God sent an angel to Joseph personally, so he could be assured of the truth of Mary's story.

So as you struggle with your own doubts, remember that God is not offended. He asks only that you seek Him and feed on His Word so that your faith can continue to grow.

My Precious Child:

Jesus once said to a father seeking help for his child, "If you can believe, all things are possible to him who believes" (Mark 9:23 NKJV). Anyone can believe for a second or two. It's only when you have the tenacity to hold on and keep believing despite the negative circumstances that you truly receive the results you're looking for.

Imagine doubt and faith on a set of scales. As you focus on your doubts, the scale tips in their favor. But if on the other side of the scale you put faith—believing you have received the desired outcome regardless of circumstances to the contrary—the scale tips in your favor.

Think positively. Believe My Word. See yourself on the other side of the mountain you are facing, victoriously overcoming doubt and possessing all that you've asked for.

Your loving Father

Dreams

The Lord said,
"Before I formed you in the womb I knew you,
before you were born I set you apart."

JEREMIAH 1:5

God said, "I know what I'm doing. I have it all planned out—
plans to take care of you, not abandon you, plans to give you
the future you hope for."

JEREMIAH 29:11 MSG

As it is written:
"No eye has seen,
no ear has heard,
no mind has conceived
what God has prepared for those who love him"—
but God has revealed it to us by his Spirit.

1 CORINTHIANS 2:9-10

The path of the righteous is like the light of dawn,
which shines brighter and brighter until full day.

PROVERBS 4:18 RSV

GOD'S GREATEST DREAM FOR YOU

Did you know that God has great dreams for you? When you were still being formed in your mother's womb, He saw you and knew you and loved you. Even then He was working on big plans designed specifically for you—plans that will give you great hope and a bright future! He made you special—one of a kind, unique—and has given you talents, abilities, passions, and gifts that are all your own.

Do you know all the good things He wants for you? He longs for you to know Him and to know how much He loves you. He wants that love to overflow so that you can't help but share it with other people He wants to reach.

God wants to fill your life with a joy so deep that nothing can take it away. His heart's desire is to flood your heart with a peace that will help you withstand anything that the world throws at you. He wishes for you to have great patience so that you can wait on His best for you. He wants to fill you with kindness so that He might use you to love His other children. He dreams that you will be faithful to Him all your days so that His blessings can flow freely into your life.

These are His dreams for you now as you graduate and for all your days to come. You are so precious to Him, and if you'll keep your heart open and give Him first place in your life, He'll make these dreams, and many more, come true.

Encouragement

Anxious hearts are very heavy
but a word of encouragement does wonders!
PROVERBS 12:25 TLB

Encourage one another daily, as long as it is called Today,
so that none of you may be hardened by sin's deceitfulness.
HEBREWS 3:13

Encourage each other. Live in harmony and peace.
2 CORINTHIANS 13:11 NLT

The LORD your God has given you the land.
Go up and take possession of it as the LORD, the God of your
fathers, told you. Do not be afraid; do not be discouraged.
DEUTERONOMY 1:21

With each of you we were like a father with his child,
holding your hand, whispering encouragement, showing you
step-by-step how to live well before God, who called us into his own
kingdom, into this delightful life.
1 THESSALONIANS 2:11-12 MSG

Let us try to do what makes peace and helps one another.
ROMANS 14:19 NCV

GOD'S ENCOURAGEMENT LIFELINES

As you enter this new era in your life as a graduate, you are going to find discouragement coming at you from all sides. You may face rejection in your job search or even in new relationships you are trying to form. The natural uncertainty that comes with big changes can be unnerving and frustrating. Everything is different, and while new can be exciting, it can also be discouraging.

The good news is that, just as discouragement can come at you in many different ways, encouragement can be found all around you as well. First, God has given you an entire book full of His words of encouragement through the Bible. If you'll take some time each day to let Him build you up, you'll find it easier and easier to put discouragement aside and face new challenges with optimism.

In addition to the Bible, God has also placed people in your life to be sources of encouragement for you when you need it most. When you're struggling, don't go it alone. Make it a top priority to develop and maintain a few truly intimate relationships. When you share your discouragement with your parents, friends, or even your pastor, God will use their words to lift you up and give you the strength to forge ahead.

So when you find yourself bogged down in the mire of discouragement, remember that God has provided you with lifelines. Reach out to Him, to His Word, and to the people He has placed in your life. When you do, He will be faithful to pull you out of even the darkest times and into the light of His love and encouragement.

Entertainment

Their trust should be in the living God,
who richly gives us all we need for our enjoyment.

1 TIMOTHY 6:17 NLT

Whatever is true, whatever is noble, whatever is right,
whatever is pure, whatever is lovely, whatever is admirable—
if anything is excellent or praiseworthy—think about such things.

PHILIPPIANS 4:8

Above all else, guard your heart,
for it is the wellspring of life.

PROVERBS 4:23

Give me your heart, my son,
And let your eyes delight in my ways.

PROVERBS 23:26 NASB

There is nothing better for mortals than to eat and drink,
and find enjoyment in their toil. This also, I saw,
is from the hand of God; for apart from him who can eat or
who can have enjoyment?

ECCLESIASTES 2:24-25 NRSV

Heavenly Father:

It's so nice after a long, hard week to kick back and be entertained by movies, video games, the Internet, or music. I know it's okay to relax, but sometimes I can become numb to the danger lurking within certain forms of entertainment. A movie may seem harmless at the onset, but before I know it, images are flashing before me that I know are not pleasing to You.

I realize that it is important to guard my heart because my very life springs from it. Help me to quickly recognize the dangers that try to seduce me. My thoughts need to be on You and not held prisoner to the images of darkness.

Help me discern those types of entertainment that will compromise my values or jeopardize my relationship with You.

Amen.

EXCELLENT ENTERTAINMENT

Today your entertainment choices are nearly limitless. The world is full of fun and interesting things to watch, play, read, and listen to. Unfortunately, it is also full of many destructive things that are disguised as harmless entertainment. Now that you have graduated, you are responsible for what you allow into your heart and mind.

God has provided a handy guide to help you make wise decisions about entertainment. Here are some questions taken from the principles in God's Word that can help you make healthy choices when it comes to how you spend your leisure time:

- Does this movie, game, song, etc., give me a glimpse of truth, or is it trying to make a lie sound like truth? For example, does this movie show that there are consequences for evil acts, or does it make evil seem cool and attractive?
- Does this form of entertainment promote ideals that are noble, such as being generous, showing kindness, and loving others?
- Is watching, playing, or listening to this media right, in and of itself? For example, pornography is morally wrong and should be avoided at all costs.
- Does this entertainment compromise my purity? Will it cause me to displease God?
- Is this form of entertainment beautiful, admirable, and excellent? Does it cause me to thank God?

God has created our world for us to enjoy. He wants us to find pleasure and joy, and entertainment is one of His blessings to us. When you choose according to God's guidelines, you will find that you're not only entertained, you're also enriched by the goodness of God's wonderful creativity.

My Precious Child:

You've heard it said that you are what you eat. Well, the same is true regarding what you think!

Your thoughts play a huge role in determining the direction your life will go. Your eyes and ears are the gateways to your spirit and soul. What you allow to pass through them influences you, whether you realize it or not.

As a graduate, you will be exposed to things you've never experienced before. You may not have to answer to your parents, but that places a big responsibility on you. This is why it is so important that you stay filled up with My Word. Only then will you have the discernment you need to make wise choices and the strength to resist temptation.

Good, clean entertainment is sometimes difficult to find, but it's out there. Trust Me, and I will lead you to it.

Your loving Father

Eternal Life

Jesus said, "I came so they can have real and eternal life,
more and better life than they ever dreamed of."
JOHN 10:10 MSG

Jesus said, "Those who drink of the water that I will give them
will never be thirsty. The water that I will give will become
in them a spring of water gushing up to eternal life."
JOHN 4:14 NRSV

Jesus said, "This is eternal life: that they may know you,
the only true God, and Jesus Christ, whom you have sent."
JOHN 17:3

Jesus said, "Very truly, I tell you, anyone who hears my word and
believes him who sent me has eternal life, and does not come under
judgment, but has passed from death to life."
JOHN 5:24 NRSV

This is the testimony: God gave us eternal life, and this life is in
his Son. Whoever has the Son has life; whoever does not have the
Son of God does not have life.
1 JOHN 5:11-12 NRSV

LIVING FOREVER, HERE AND NOW

With your diploma in hand and your future stretching out before you, the idea of eternal life probably doesn't cross your mind too much. After all, eternal life is for after you die, right?

If this is your perception, you may be surprised to learn that everlasting life actually starts here and now. When Jesus came to live on earth, He didn't just give us instructions on how to get to heaven. He spent much of His time explaining how to start living in the kingdom of God long before this life is over.

How can you start your eternal life right now? The first step is to accept it as a gift from God by believing that Jesus gave His life for you. When Jesus died on the cross, He cancelled out all the things in your life that have kept you from God. No matter what you've done, He has forgiven you and cleansed you. When you believe that and ask God to make it real in your heart, you begin living eternal life right then and there!

Once you've taken that step, you can begin kingdom living by reading God's Word and talking to Him in prayer. Through these activities, God will begin showing you the great purpose He has for your life. And as you discover this purpose and fulfill it, you will not only be preparing yourself for eternal life in heaven, you'll be free to start living it right now.

So don't put it off. Become a child of God. As you live for Him, He will place heaven in your heart, even while you're still on earth.

Expectations

My soul, wait silently for God alone,
For my expectation is from Him.

PSALM 62:5 NKJV

To Him who is able to do exceedingly abundantly above all that
we ask or think, according to the power that works in us,
to Him be glory in the church by Christ Jesus.

EPHESIANS 3:20-21 NKJV

The Lord says,
"Anyone who trusts in me will not be disappointed."

ISAIAH 49:23 NCV

The Lord GOD says:
"I will put a stone in the ground in Jerusalem,
a tested stone. Everything will be built on this important
and precious rock. Anyone who trusts in it
will never be disappointed."

ISAIAH 28:16 NCV

As for me, I will watch expectantly for the LORD;
I will wait for the God of my salvation.

MICAH 7:7 NASB

GREATER EXPECTATIONS

Andrew had great expectations for his life after graduation. He had worked hard, graduated with honors, and now he was ready to make his dreams come true—he was heading to California to pursue a career in filmmaking. He wanted to make great movies that would change people's lives. With a noble cause like that as his goal, Andrew was sure that God would make it happen.

Andrew arrived in California and began writing screenplays and searching out studio contacts. He continued to expect his big break to come along any day, even after a year of rejections. But after two years, Andrew felt discouragement setting in. He had been so sure of his plan. Why wasn't God making it happen?

With a heart full of disappointment and a head full of confusion, Andrew joined a small Bible study group at the church he'd been attending occasionally. He needed answers. Andrew soon began to realize that his expectations for his future had been his alone. He hadn't asked God for guidance—he'd simply hoped that God would go along with his plan.

And so, Andrew began to seriously pray for direction. The answers came slowly but surely. Opportunities began to open up for him to use his creativity to help various ministries. With each new project, his passion for using words and images to illustrate God's love grew. He began to realize that God did have a great purpose for him and his writing—a purpose that was even greater than his expectations.

When you face disappointment, remember that God hasn't abandoned you. He may be showing you that He has something better in store for you than you had planned for yourself.

Faith

Jesus said to them, ". . . For truly, I say to you, if you have faith
as a grain of mustard seed, you will say to this mountain,
'Move from here to there,' and it will move; and nothing
will be impossible to you."

MATTHEW 17:20 RSV

What is faith? It is the confident assurance that what we hope for is
going to happen. It is the evidence of things we cannot yet see.

HEBREWS 11:1 NLT

[Abraham] did not waver at the promise of God through unbelief,
but was strengthened in faith, giving glory to God, and being fully
convinced that what He had promised He was also able to perform.

ROMANS 4:20-21 NKJV

We live by faith, not by sight.

2 CORINTHIANS 5:7

We must always give thanks to God for you, brothers and sisters,
as is right, because your faith is growing abundantly.

2 THESSALONIANS 1:3 NRSV

Heavenly Father:

My world is so full of an I'll-believe-it-when-I-see-it mentality that sometimes it is hard to trust in You and the things I cannot see. I know that requires faith.

I want to be a person who trusts You with my whole heart. Help me recognize when doubts try to sneak in and help me seal up the crevices of my heart so they can't take root.

I know the key is found in Your Word. Give me a deeper desire to study it so that my faith will grow and be anchored in You. I want to have the faith that Jesus talked about, the faith that can move mountains.

Amen.

WHAT IS FAITH?

Faith is a word you hear a lot today. Many people equate it with being religious or spiritual. Some think it means to have confidence in yourself—"Have faith and you can accomplish anything." But what does faith really mean?

The Bible gives us many examples of what it means to truly have faith. Here are just a few and some ways that they apply to you:

- Faith is trusting that God will keep His promises in spite of all appearances to the contrary. This might mean believing that God has great plans for your life, even when you're working in a dead-end job.
- Faith is doing what you know God wants you to do, even when you are scared. God might be telling you very clearly that you need to move or take a new job. If you'll take that first step of faith, even when you're really frightened, God will bless you for your obedience with more faith, guidance, and strength.
- Faith is believing that even the impossible is possible through God's power. Maybe you have a big dream—one that just won't go away in spite of the fact that you think it can never come true. God may be asking you to have faith in the impossible so that He can bring it to pass.

Simply put, faith is trusting that God is who He says He is and that He will do what He promises to do. Having faith isn't easy, but Jesus says that even the tiniest bit of it can do the impossible. So hold on to even the littlest seed of faith, and watch it grow as you trust in God.

My Precious Child:

I have given you My Son Jesus, the author and finisher of your faith. As you read about His time on earth, you will see many demonstrations of faith. He stands ready to help you develop yours.

Be confident that the faith you have is adequate. It is a credit to you that you believe in Me without ever having seen Me, for that requires a high level of trust.

As you continue to discover My character and nature, you will find your spirit growing stronger and stronger. At the same time, you will find your faith growing right along with it. If you continue to feed your faith and apply it to areas of your life, what started out as small as a mustard seed will indeed move any mountain that stands in your way.

Your loving Father

Fear

I call to you from the ends of the earth
when I am afraid.
Carry me away to a high mountain.
You have been my protection,
like a strong tower against my enemies.

PSALM 61:2-3 NCV

I am the LORD, your God,
who takes hold of your right hand
and says to you, Do not fear;
I will help you.

ISAIAH 41:13

Don't be afraid, for I am with you.
Do not be dismayed, for I am your God.
I will strengthen you. I will help you.
I will uphold you with my victorious right hand.

ISAIAH 41:10 NLT

When I am afraid, I will put my confidence in you.
Yes, I will trust the promises of God.

PSALM 56:3-4 TLB

A CURE FOR EVERY FEAR

Fear is natural, especially for you as a recent graduate facing new challenges and an uncertain future. But if you let fear consume you, it can act like a disease, paralyzing you, making you sick spiritually and physically, and keeping you from healthy growth. The good news is that God, the Great Healer, has the remedy for all your fears:

- When people or situations threaten to destroy you, God promises you deliverance.
- When you face danger—physically, mentally, or spiritually— God promises you protection.
- When loneliness and isolation fill you with fear, God promises to be with you.
- When you fear that you can never be forgiven, God promises you salvation.
- When you are afraid that you are too weak to go on, God promises you His strength.
- When the task ahead of you is overwhelming, God promises to be your helper.
- When you feel unloved and worthless, God promises to love you unconditionally.
- When you're confused and uncertain, God promises to give you wisdom.
- When life fills you with despair so that you fear for your future, God promises to bring you hope.
- When you feel like you are a slave to your fears, God promises to free you.

For every fear, God promises a cure. Run to Him like a child running to a loving daddy, and you will find peace in His arms.

Forgiveness

If we confess our sins, He is faithful and just to forgive us our sins
and to cleanse us from all unrighteousness.

1 JOHN 1:9 NKJV

"Come now, let us reason together," says the LORD.
"Though your sins are like scarlet,
they shall be as white as snow;
though they are red as crimson,
they shall be like wool."

ISAIAH 1:18

As far as the east is from the west,
So far has He removed our transgressions from us.

PSALM 103:12 NASB

I am still not all I should be but I am bringing all my energies to
bear on this one thing: Forgetting the past and looking forward to
what lies ahead, I strain to reach the end of the race and receive the
prize for which God is calling us up to heaven because of what
Christ Jesus did for us.

PHILIPPIANS 3:13-14 TLB

PUTTING THE PAST IN THE PAST

The past sometimes haunts us. We struggle to put it behind us, but it keeps whispering, telling us that we'll never be forgiven. As you graduate and start your adult life, you may find that your past mistakes make it difficult for you to move ahead. If so, God wants to encourage you with the story of eleven young people who struggled with the same problem.

Jesus chose a group of young men, probably only in their teens or early twenties, to be His disciples. They spent nearly every minute of three whole years with Jesus. They became closer than brothers. Yet when Jesus was arrested and executed, just the time when He needed His best friends the most, they all deserted Him.

These young people made huge mistakes. They were probably afraid that they had messed up too much for God to ever forgive them. But in spite of their failures, when Jesus came back to life, He appeared to His young friends and didn't hesitate to forgive them all. With the reassurance that their mistakes had been erased, these young men put their past behind them and became powerful servants of God. They healed people, started churches, and faced persecution bravely. God's forgiveness didn't just erase their past mistakes—it changed their lives forever.

Jesus wants to do the same for you today. Your past missteps can be erased when you offer them to God and ask for His forgiveness. When you ask, He promises to wipe your life clean and give you a new start.

Freedom

It is absolutely clear that God has called you to a free life.
Just make sure that you don't use this freedom as an excuse to do
whatever you want to do and destroy your freedom.
Rather, use your freedom to serve one another in love;
that's how freedom grows.

GALATIANS 5:13 MSG

Jesus said, "If the Son makes you free, you will be free indeed."

JOHN 8:36 RSV

We know that our old life died with Christ on the cross so that our
sinful selves would have no power over us and we would not be slaves
to sin. Anyone who has died is made free from sin's control.

ROMANS 6:6-7 NCV

Jesus said, "If you continue in my word, you are truly my disciples,
and you will know the truth, and the truth will make you free."

JOHN 8:31-32 RSV

Now you are free from the power of sin and are slaves of God,
and his benefits to you include holiness and everlasting life.

ROMANS 6:22 TLB

Heavenly Father:

It feels so good to finally be through with school! I am celebrating my newfound freedom, but I am finding it tempting to do things that are a little edgy and push the envelope. I want to make good choices that will propel me toward what You have planned for me, but I also want to explore so many things that I've never done before.

Some things are clearly right or wrong, but what about the gray areas? How can I know if some of those things are okay? I couldn't wait to be on my own, but now I'm finding it to be a huge responsibility that sometimes overwhelms me.

Guide me as I read Your Word, and speak to my heart. Help me to make wise choices that will please You and will enable me to live in true freedom.

Amen.

I'M FREE

With a joyful toss of your mortarboard, you announce to the world, "I'm free!" Now you get to make your own choices and do your own thing. Your new freedom is exhilarating and full of wonderful possibilities.

With freedom, though, comes great responsibility—and even some danger. Some choices that may seem liberating at first glance might actually take away your freedom. For example, hitting the clubs and enjoying the alcohol that flows so freely there might seem like a good time—a formerly forbidden activity that you're now free to explore. But if you're not careful, you could end up a slave to the guilt and regret that all too often accompany a night of partying. Maybe you've been told from an early age to save your money, but now you're free to get that credit card and splurge on some of those things you've always wanted. All too soon, though, the bill will come in the mail, and you'll find yourself in the trap of debt.

Contrary to what the world tells you, true freedom is actually found through obedience. God has provided you with the Bible—full of guidelines for living a truly free life. When you do what He calls you to do, even when it isn't easy, you'll find yourself living a life free of the bondage of guilt, regret, and discouragement that poor choices can bring.

So embrace your new freedom. Try new things, meet new people, and enjoy the privileges that come with being an adult. With God's Word as your guide, you'll be able to wake up each morning and with true joy declare, "I'm free!"

My Precious Child:

With freedom come choices and with choices, great responsibility. Freedom allows you to take risks and explore your boundaries. A word of caution, though—don't step over into areas where you know you shouldn't.

As My child, you know in your heart what is and is not pleasing to Me. Understand that My hand of protection only extends within the boundaries of obedience. When you venture beyond them, you step out from under My covering. You are responsible for your choices, and you will reap the consequences of your actions.

Listen to the voice of wisdom as you explore your new freedoms. Make decisions based upon My Word. It's more black-and-white than you think. Listen to My voice and follow My direction. My path is one of great adventure on the path of righteous obedience. Let's explore your destiny together.

Your loving Father

Friendship

Jesus said, "This is my commandment, that you love one another
as I have loved you. No one has greater love than this,
to lay down one's life for one's friends."

JOHN 15:12-13 NRSV

Disregarding another person's faults preserves love;
telling about them separates close friends.

PROVERBS 17:9 NLT

Confess your sins to each other and pray for each other
so that you may be healed.

JAMES 5:16 NLT

A friend loveth at all times.

PROVERBS 17:17 KJV

As iron sharpens iron, a friend sharpens a friend.

PROVERBS 27:17 NLT

The eye cannot say to the hand, "I have no need of you,"
nor again the head to the feet, "I have no need of you."
On the contrary, the parts of the body which seem
to be weaker are indispensable.

1 CORINTHIANS 12:21-22 RSV

TRUE FRIENDSHIP

Good friendship is one of the best things in life. As you prepared to graduate, you probably spent time reminiscing with your friends about all the good times you had together. You're probably a little sad, too, realizing that your relationships are going to change as you each pursue your lives in the "real world." Inevitably you will lose touch with some friends, while your relationships with others will stay strong. And as you begin a new chapter in your life, you'll find new friends too.

Whether you're working to keep old friendships strong or looking to forge new ones, God has given you some great guidance in His Word for finding and keeping good friends:

- Be the kind of friend you would want to have.
- Seek out wise people to be your best friends.
- Realize that your best friends don't just tell you what you want to hear. They tell you the truth, even when it hurts.
- The truest friends are those who encourage you in your friendship with Jesus.
- Put your friends' interests ahead of your own.
- Taking time to worship and serve God together will create lifelong bonds that nothing can sever.
- Sharing your weaknesses and struggles with your friends and praying together about them will make you and your friends stronger.
- Be truly happy when your friends succeed and genuinely concerned when they face struggles.
- Be willing to ask for and accept help from each other— trying to go it alone weakens friendships.
- Make Jesus your very best friend, and His love will flow to all your other friendships, strengthening them even more.

Fun

I recommend having fun, because there is nothing better
for people to do in this world than to eat, drink, and enjoy life.
That way they will experience some happiness along with
all the hard work God gives them.

ECCLESIASTES 8:15 NLT

The young girls will dance for joy, and men folk—old and young—
will take their part in all the fun; for I will turn their mourning into
joy and I will comfort them and make them rejoice.

JEREMIAH 31:13 TLB

My soul will rejoice in the LORD
and delight in his salvation.

PSALM 35:9

A merry heart makes a cheerful countenance. . . .
He who is of a merry heart has a continual feast.

PROVERBS 15:13,15 NKJV

Rejoice in the LORD, you who do right.
Praise his holy name.

PSALM 97:12 NCV

THE CREATOR OF FUN

As a new graduate, set aside a day to celebrate and have some fun with your Creator. Yes, have some fun with God!

Start the day with a bowl of fresh strawberries for breakfast—He made them bright red and really sweet, just to tickle your taste buds. Next, head outside. Look at the beautiful blue hue with which He painted the sky. And those big, white clouds. As He causes the wind to make them change shape, lie on the grass and see what formations you can make out. Do you see a bear, the profile of an old man, a sailboat?

Next, why not play a game of fetch with your dog? Domesticated animals make fine furry friends, and they're a lot of fun, too—just one more way that God has chosen to say, "I love you."

Later, meet your best friend for coffee. God loves it when you enjoy life with others. He can't help but smile as He observes the two of you laughing until you cry.

In the early evening, be sure to check out the special sunset that He paints just for you. Then hang around a little longer to witness the beautiful display of stars and possibly a meteor shower. He loves to wow you with His handiwork.

Whether you choose to do it today or another day in the near future, take some time to be with God, to have fun and enjoy the many blessings He has created for you. It will bring joy to His heart and will delight your heart too.

Giving

Each of you must give as you have made up your mind,
not reluctantly or under compulsion, for God loves a cheerful
giver. And God is able to provide you with every blessing
in abundance, so that by always having enough of everything,
you may share abundantly in every good work.

2 CORINTHIANS 9:7-8 NRSV

It is possible to give freely and become more wealthy, but those
who are stingy will lose everything. The generous prosper and are
satisfied; those who refresh others will themselves be refreshed.

PROVERBS 11:24-25 NLT

Those who in the present age are rich, command them not to be
haughty, or to set their hopes on the uncertainty of riches,
but rather on God who richly provides us with everything for our
enjoyment. They are to do good, to be rich in good works,
generous, and ready to share, thus storing up for themselves the
treasure of a good foundation for the future, so that they
may take hold of the life that really is life.

1 TIMOTHY 6:17-19 NRSV

Jesus said, "If you give, you will receive. Your gift will return to you
in full measure, pressed down, shaken together to make room
for more, and running over."

LUKE 6:38 NLT

Heavenly Father:

I'm just starting out. I don't have a lot to give at this point, but what I have is Yours. You've given me so much more than I could ever repay. Show me how to be generous with all of it, to give from a pure and willing heart.

Forgive me, Lord, when I give out of wrong motives, when I feel embarrassed or intimidated or when I am just eager to please others. Remind me often that it's a heart of obedience that You have promised to bless.

On the other hand, Lord, give me a nudge when I'm slow to hear You speak to me or when I am insensitive to the needs around me. Chase greed and selfishness from my heart and mind, and fill me with Your good and generous Spirit.

Amen.

THE GENEROUS WIDOW

Jesus and His disciples sit in a loose circle in the court of the temple. Those passing by note the group with interest. "Isn't that the Teacher everyone has been talking about?" one woman asks another.

A few surprised gasps rise from the crowd as the Teacher pans the religious scholars for their academic arrogance and addiction to public flattery and their exploitation of the weak and helpless.

Then Jesus notices a woman making her way through the crowd. Judging by her beleaguered appearance, she is a widow— one of the lowest rungs on the social ladder. All eyes turn to see what has captured the Teacher's attention. But they quickly shrug their shoulders and turn back to Jesus. The beggarly woman is all but invisible to their eyes.

Slowly, but with determination, the widow makes her way forward and drops her small coins into one of the collection plates. The crowd waits quietly for the Teacher to speak, but only the jingling of change can be heard as the rich drop their generous contributions into the wooden plates.

As the widow turns to leave, she sees the Teacher pointing in her direction.

"I tell you the truth," He says, "this poor widow has put in more than all the others. All these people gave their gifts out of their wealth; but she out of her poverty put in all she had to live on" (Luke 21:3-4).

As you head into the next phase of your life, how much you give to God and to others in His name will be your decision alone. God doesn't ask that you give everything you have, but He does want you to give in the spirit of the generous widow— willingly, determinedly, and from the heart.

My Precious Child:

I hear your words, and I see your heart. I know you have little to give right now. But remember that the amount you give is far less important than the way you give—willingly and cheerfully. When you give from a pure heart, I bless and multiply your gifts to enrich the lives of many. Your gift, however small, will also be used to bless you again—providing increasing abundance to meet your needs and allow you to give even more generously.

As you look to the future and begin to travel the path I've set before you, being generous with others is one of the greatest investments you can make. Open your heart and your hand, and I promise that I will pour out My blessings upon you.

Your loving Father

God's Faithfulness

I face your Temple as I worship, giving thanks to you for all your
lovingkindness and your faithfulness, for your promises are backed
by all the honor of your name.

PSALM 138:2 TLB

Lord, you are a God who shows mercy and is kind.
You don't become angry quickly.
You have great love and faithfulness.

PSALM 86:15 NCV

All the paths of the LORD are steadfast love and faithfulness,
for those who keep his covenant and his testimonies.

PSALM 25:10 RSV

Your love, O LORD, reaches to the heavens,
your faithfulness to the skies.

PSALM 36:5

Great is his steadfast love toward us;
and the faithfulness of the LORD endures for ever.

PSALM 117:2 RSV

HE'LL NEVER LET YOU DOWN

Your boss said that your promotion was a sure thing—until this morning when he announced that the job had gone to someone else. Your best friend was supposed to be moving in next week—you had so many great plans for your new apartment—but at the last minute she changed her mind and decided to take a job out of state. Now you're left with shattered plans and a rent too big for your budget. Your parents had always seemed so solid. They had always promised you that divorce was not an option for them. Yet now here you are, spending your first holiday with your dad and new stepmother.

People are going to let you down. As a graduate in the adult world, you are probably realizing, more than ever before, that humans have trouble with faithfulness. You've probably already been disappointed more than once by people you trust, even by people who love you.

It's easy to get discouraged in the face of unfaithfulness. You may even find yourself struggling to trust God. But, thankfully, you can count on Him to be faithful—no matter what. In fact, God is actually incapable of breaking a promise! An essential part of His very being is that He is faithful and trustworthy. When He makes you a promise, you don't ever have to worry about being let down or betrayed.

So when you're faced with the unfaithfulness of others, turn to your faithful Father. He promises over and over in His Word that He will never leave you or forsake you. When you put your full trust in Him, you will never be disappointed.

God's Love

Praise the LORD, O my soul,
and forget not all his benefits . . .
who redeems your life from the pit
and crowns you with love and compassion.

PSALM 103:2,4

God shows his great love for us in this way:
Christ died for us while we were still sinners.

ROMANS 5:8 NCV

The LORD passed in front of Moses and said, "I am the LORD.
The LORD is a God who shows mercy, who is kind, who doesn't
become angry quickly, who has great love and faithfulness and
is kind to thousands of people. The LORD forgives people for evil,
for sin, and for turning against him."

EXODUS 34:6-7 NCV

The LORD shows mercy and is kind.
He does not become angry quickly, and he has great love.

PSALM 103:8 NCV

God is love. This is how God showed his love to us:
He sent his one and only Son into the world so that
we could have life through him.

1 JOHN 4:8-9 NCV

GOD'S UNFATHOMABLE LOVE

You've probably been told that God is love and that God loves you. These are both really nice concepts, but what do they really mean? How does God's love apply to your life and all that you are going to face as a graduate?

When you take a look at what the Bible has to say about the depth of God's love, you'll find that it is beyond anything you could ever imagine. His love is described as unfailing, better than life, abundant, faithful, everlasting, and comforting. God's love is like powerful wings that hide you from danger. It's like a strong fortress. It lifts you up when you are about to fall.

God's love makes you special. He actually crowns you with it! The Bible says that this amazing love reaches to the heavens, fills the earth, endures forever, and is better than pure gold.

God proved His love for you when He sent Jesus, His beloved Son, to die on earth and be raised again. Through Jesus, God broke down all the barriers that separated you from Him so that you can know the incredible depth of His love.

God loves you more than even your most trusted and beloved friend or family member. His love doesn't depend on anything you do for Him. He loves you because He simply cannot help but love you; He is love. As you begin this new chapter in your life, take this love with you and know that no matter where you go, you'll always be unconditionally loved.

God's Will

Be joyful always; pray continually; give thanks in all circumstances,
for this is God's will for you in Christ Jesus.

1 THESSALONIANS 5:16-18

Do not conform any longer to the pattern of this world,
but be transformed by the renewing of your mind.
Then you will be able to test and approve what God's will is—
his good, pleasing and perfect will.

ROMANS 12:2

The Holy Spirit helps us with our daily problems and
in our praying. For we don't even know what we should pray for,
nor how to pray as we should; but the Holy Spirit . . .
pleads for us in harmony with God's own will.

ROMANS 8:26-27 TLB

Let the peace (soul harmony which comes) from Christ rule
(act as umpire continually) in your hearts [deciding and settling
with finality all questions that arise in your minds].

COLOSSIANS 3:15 AMP

Jesus said, "The sheep hear [a shepherd's] voice and come to him;
and he calls his own sheep by name and leads them out.
He walks ahead of them; and they follow him,
for they recognize his voice. . . . I am the Good Shepherd."

JOHN 10:3-4,11 TLB

Heavenly Father:

I believe You have great plans for me. Your Word says so. And I don't want to miss out on anything You have planned. I desire to please You in everything I do. I want You to be proud of me as I live according to the dreams You've placed in my heart.

Tell me where to go, what to do, and when to do it; and I will obey. I trust the Holy Spirit to be my guide. Help me to follow Him closely, so I won't miss a beat.

Thank You, Father, for the opportunities You bring into my life for success. Speak to my heart and help me to realize every single one of them. I choose Your way, Lord, because I know it is the right way for me!

Amen.

SOLVING THE MYSTERY
OF GOD'S WILL

You did it—you're finally a graduate! The future stretches out before you, full of possibility. You've heard a lot about following God's will for your life, and while that sounds like a good thing to do, how do you know what God's will is? God doesn't seem to be sending angelic messengers much these days, so how can you really know which job He wants you to take or where you should live?

Finding God's will can seem very mysterious, but God doesn't hide His will from you. In fact, He has clearly spelled out in the Bible how you can please Him with your life. When you follow His guidelines for living, He will begin to reveal to you the specific plans He has for your future.

First, love God above everything else. Make knowing Him and obeying Him your top priorities. When you do, you'll start to hear His voice more clearly through reading the Bible, spending time in prayer, and listening to the advice of wise friends. God will also assure you that you are making the right choices by blessing you with a deep sense of peace.

Second, God's will is that you love other people as much as you love yourself. When you're trying to make a big decision, remember to take the interests of others into account. While you can't please everyone all the time, being sensitive to the needs of others and making choices based on selflessness, rather than selfishness, will always please God.

When you seek to follow these basics of God's will, He will never fail to bless you with specific wisdom and guidance for your own personal choices.

My Precious Child:

My will is not a mystery that's been hidden from you, and discovering it shouldn't be a struggle. I desire for you to know My purpose for your life so you can live that purpose to the full. I give you wisdom as you ask for it, and I guide you. Confusion is not from Me.

One of the main reasons I have given you the Holy Spirit is so that He will guide you into all truth. He speaks to your heart what He hears from Me, and He declares to you the things to come. Each day the road to your destiny becomes brighter and brighter as you follow His instruction.

I'm so excited about our journey. I've seen your end from the beginning and it's exciting! As you step out, know that we're doing this together.

Your loving Father

God's Word

God's words will always prove true and right,
no matter who questions them.

ROMANS 3:4 TLB

Your words are what sustain me; they are food to my hungry soul.
They bring joy to my sorrowing heart and delight me.

JEREMIAH 15:16 TLB

I treasure your word in my heart,
so that I may not sin against you.

PSALM 119:11 NRSV

The Lord said, "This book of the law shall not depart from
your mouth, but you shall meditate on it day and night,
so that you may be careful to do according to all that is written in it;
for then you will make your way prosperous,
and then you will have success."

JOSHUA 1:8 NASB

The word of God is living and active, sharper than any
two-edged sword, piercing until it divides soul from spirit,
joints from marrow; it is able to judge the thoughts and
intentions of the heart.

HEBREWS 4:12 NRSV

GETTING THE MOST
OUT OF GOD'S WORD

Now that you have graduated, studying is probably the last thing on your mind. But as you begin life on your own, with all its challenges and decisions, studying God's Word is vital to give you direction, guidance, and encouragement. Here are a few tips on how to get the most out of your Bible:

- Take some time to find a Bible version that is easy to read and that has good study notes, maps, and devotional readings to help you understand and apply what you're reading.
- Do your best to read your Bible every day, even if it's for only a few minutes, so that it becomes a habit.
- Don't feel like you have to read a certain amount every day. If something really speaks to you, take the time you need to think and pray about it until you really understand what God is saying.
- Keep a journal handy and jot down the things you learn, the things you don't understand, and your prayers.
- Find a mentor, someone who has been studying the Bible for a while and who has wisdom to share. Try to meet regularly to study together. Ask lots of questions. Other believers are one of the gifts God gives us to help us grow in our relationship with Him.

God's Word is powerful and full of wisdom. When you make Bible reading a daily part of your life, you'll be blessed with the answers you need to face your new future with confidence and true joy.

Grace

If your life honors the name of Jesus, he will honor you.
Grace is behind and through all of this, our God giving himself
freely, the Master, Jesus Christ, giving himself freely.

2 THESSALONIANS 1:12 MSG

Even though on the outside it often looks like things are falling
apart on us, on the inside, where God is making new life,
not a day goes by without his unfolding grace.

2 CORINTHIANS 4:16 MSG

Now God has us where he wants us, with all the time in this world
and the next to shower grace and kindness upon us in Christ Jesus.

EPHESIANS 2:7 MSG

From his fullness we have all received, grace upon grace.
The law indeed was given through Moses; grace and truth came
through Jesus Christ.

JOHN 1:16-17 NRSV

The amazing grace of the Master, Jesus Christ, the extravagant love
of God, the intimate friendship of the Holy Spirit,
be with all of you.

2 CORINTHIANS 13:14 MSG

A LESSON FROM A LLAMA

A few years ago, Disney released a movie called *The Emperor's New Groove* about a selfish emperor named Kuzco who decides to demolish a whole village in order to build himself a new palace. One of the villagers, a man named Pacha, begs the emperor to consider all the lives he will be destroying. But Kuzco doesn't care about anyone but himself. Before the emperor can carry out his plans, though, his advisor turns him into a llama so she can assume the throne.

Kuzco is tied up and tossed outside of the palace walls where Pacha, who is dejectedly making his way home, finds him. In spite of Kuzco's terrible selfishness, Pacha frees him and then risks his life to help him retake the throne.

What looks like a silly cartoon on the surface is actually a powerful story of grace. Just like Kuzco, all of us are born selfish and in dire need of help to be restored to what we were created to be. Just when we find ourselves at our most desperate state and in bondage because of our own mistakes, God sends Jesus to rescue us.

Just as Kuzco didn't deserve Pacha's help, none of us deserve God's love and salvation. But that is what grace means— undeserved favor. Out of God's goodness, and not because of anything that we have done, He rescues us and restores us when we accept His grace.

As you begin this new chapter in your life after graduation, may you be filled with joy and awe at God's amazing grace. No matter what you've done, He loves you and wants to give you a new life through Jesus.

Guidance

Your word is a lamp for my feet
and a light for my path.

PSALM 119:105 NLT

Let the peace (soul harmony which comes) from Christ rule
(act as umpire continually) in your hearts [deciding and settling
with finality all questions that arise in your minds].

COLOSSIANS 3:15 AMP

You will hear a voice say, "This is the way;
turn around and walk here."

ISAIAH 30:21 NLT

The LORD says, "I will make you wise and show you where to go.
I will guide you and watch over you."

PSALM 32:8 NCV

This God is our God for ever and ever;
he will be our guide even to the end.

PSALM 48:14

The LORD of hosts . . .
Is wonderful in counsel and excellent in guidance.

ISAIAH 28:29 NKJV

Heavenly Father:

I am at a crossroads in my life, and there are so many paths to choose from. How will I ever know which one to take? I know Your plan is the place of greatest blessing for me, and I don't want to make a mistake by heading in the wrong direction. I don't want to take unnecessary detours that will end up wasting time and energy and prevent me from arriving at Your intended destination.

Sometimes the path is well lit and the road signs unmistakable. But when the way is dark and I am unsure, I need You to be my light.

You gave me Your Word as my road map for life. Let the passages I read act as landmarks along the way. And help me be at peace, confident that You are guiding my every step. Wherever You lead, I want to follow.

Amen.

THE ULTIMATE
GUIDANCE SYSTEM

Due to the wonders of modern technology, we never have to worry about getting lost again. With your handy little global positioning device, you can always know exactly where you are and how to get to where you want to go. Simply tell the device your destination, and a little voice will guide you step-by-step along the path you need to take to get there.

As a new graduate facing lots of decisions, you're probably wishing there were a handheld device that would tell you how to reach your goals. The future is full of choices, twists, and turns. How are you going to find your way? Where can you find guidance for the journey ahead?

Just like a global positioning device, God's voice will tell you exactly which way to go when you seek His guidance. When you talk to Him about your dreams and goals, He will help you know which ones to pursue. As you seek His guidance through prayer and the Bible, His still small voice will speak to your heart and show you the right way to go.

Are you trying to decide which career path to follow, where you should live, or what direction a certain relationship should take? Send a message to God through prayer, and listen for His guidance by spending time in His Word. He'll give you a sense of peace that will indicate the right turn to make.

God wants to give you guidance for every step of your journey in life. When you consult the ultimate handheld guidance system—His Word—you'll find yourself on the right road toward fulfilling your purpose and realizing your dreams.

My Precious Child:

I am pleased that you are committed to fulfilling My will, for it is the place of greatest joy. Yes,
it is important to stay on the right path, but I
don't want you to be afraid. Remember, I am
with you and in you, leading and guiding all the
way.

My Word is your road map, and I will use it to
direct your steps. Also listen for My voice and
know that it will never contradict My Word. All
My paths are peace, so when you feel uncertain
about the next step, search your heart for that
place of tranquillity. This doesn't mean that the
right way will always be easy, but there will be a
knowing, an abiding sense of peace, that you are
on the right track.

Remember, I am always with you, always
holding your hand.

Your loving Father

Guilt

Keep me from deliberate sins!
Don't let them control me.
Then I will be free of guilt
and innocent of great sin.

PSALM 19:13 NLT

There was a time when I wouldn't admit what a sinner I was.
But my dishonesty made me miserable and filled my days
with frustration. All day and all night your hand was heavy on me.
My strength evaporated like water on a sunny day until I finally
admitted all my sins to you and stopped trying to hide them.
I said to myself, "I will confess them to the Lord."
And you forgave me! All my guilt is gone.

PSALM 32:3-5 TLB

Let us draw near to God with a sincere heart in full assurance
of faith, having our hearts sprinkled to cleanse us
from a guilty conscience.

HEBREWS 10:22

What happiness for those whose guilt has been forgiven!
What joys when sins are covered over! What relief for those who have
confessed their sins and God has cleared their record.

PSALM 32:1-2 TLB

GOOD GUILT

Guilt is an emotion we all deal with from time to time. You may find that you're feeling it even more now that you're a graduate facing the demands of the "real world." Guilt never feels good, but it does serve a purpose when God uses it to show you your need for His forgiveness. Other times, though, you experience misplaced guilt that serves only to drag you down. Do you know the difference? Try this little quiz:

Which of these represent God-given guilt and which are examples of misplaced guilt?

- You're having a bad day, so you make a hurtful remark to your coworker. The more you think about it, the more you feel guilty about what you said.
- Lately you've been struggling with some doubts about God and your faith. You've been searching the Bible for answers and praying about your questions, but you feel terribly guilty for doubting God.
- A friend asks you to help him move his new couch into his apartment, but your week is packed with other commitments. You apologize and explain; but your friend is visibly disappointed, and you feel guilty.

If you picked the first as an example of "good guilt," you're right. When we do or say things that hurt others or violate God's commands, God will touch our hearts with guilt to prompt us to ask for forgiveness and make amends. This is the only purpose for guilt. Ask God to help you discern between the guilt He allows and that which is misplaced. Then act on His reminders to seek forgiveness and let the rest go.

Healthy Habits

Jesus said, "If anyone wishes to come after Me, let him deny himself, and take up his cross daily and follow Me."

LUKE 9:23 NASB

They received the word with great eagerness,
examining the Scriptures daily.

ACTS 17:11 NASB

Don't you know that you are God's temple and that God's Spirit lives in you? If anyone destroys God's temple, God will destroy that person, because God's temple is holy and you are that temple.

1 CORINTHIANS 3:16-17 NCV

Run from sex sin. No other sin affects the body as this one does. When you sin this sin it is against your own body. Haven't you yet learned that your body is the home of the Holy Spirit God gave you, and that he lives within you? Your own body does not belong to you. For God has bought you with a great price. So use every part of your body to give glory back to God, because he owns it.

1 CORINTHIANS 6:18-20 TLB

Bodily exercise profits a little, but godliness is profitable for all things, having promise of the life that now is and of that which is to come.

1 TIMOTHY 4:8 NKJV

MAKING GOD FEEL AT HOME

What would you do if God, in the flesh, came to live with you? You'd probably work a little harder to keep things clean and comfortable around your place. You'd keep the kitchen stocked with healthy food. You would think twice about what shows you watched or what books and magazines you read.

God may not be physically sitting on your couch, but if you have accepted Jesus and His forgiveness, God is actually much closer than any roommate—He lives inside you. When you become a follower of Christ, God says that you become a temple—His house. Do you want to be a spacious, sparkling-clean mansion for Him, or are you settling for being a run-down shack?

If you want to be a beautiful temple, you need to take care of yourself—mind, body, and spirit.

- Keep your mind clean by paying close attention to what you watch and read. Keep a healthy mind by spending time reading the Bible, continuing to learn and grow, and absorbing things that are good and pure.
- Keep your body healthy with good food, exercise, and rest. Taking care of yourself physically pleases God—He created your body as an incredible gift to you. When you make being healthy a priority, you are honoring God's gift.
- To have a healthy spirit, keep it clean by asking for forgiveness whenever you mess up. Feed it with God's Word, prayer, and time spent worshiping with other believers.

As you graduate and make a home for yourself, remember to also make yourself a home for God. He will bless you when you make Him welcome in your heart.

Holy Spirit

Peter said, "Change your life. Turn to God and be baptized,
each of you, in the name of Jesus Christ, so your sins are forgiven.
Receive the gift of the Holy Spirit."

ACTS 2:38 MSG

Jesus said, "I will send you the Comforter—the Holy Spirit,
the source of all truth. He will come to you from the Father and
will tell you all about me."

JOHN 15:26 TLB

Jesus said, "I will ask the Father, and he will give you another
Counselor, who will never leave you. He is the Holy Spirit,
who leads into all truth."

JOHN 14:16-17 NLT

We have not received the spirit of the world but the Spirit who is
from God, that we may understand what God has freely given us.
This is what we speak, not in words taught us by human wisdom
but in words taught by the Spirit, expressing spiritual truths
in spiritual words.

1 CORINTHIANS 2:12-13

Jesus said, "When the Father sends the Counselor as my
representative—and by the Counselor I mean the Holy Spirit—
he will teach you everything and will remind you of everything
I myself have told you."

JOHN 14:26 NLT

Heavenly Father:

The concept of the Trinity is difficult for me to grasp—God in three Persons. What does that mean?

I understand that You are my Heavenly Father, and I'm so grateful for that. I also realize that I am a sinner who needs Jesus to purchase my salvation. It is because of Him that I have been united to You. But I don't understand the Holy Spirit. What is His role?

This is confusing to me, but in Your Word, You refer to the Holy Spirit as a gift. That tells me that having Him in my life is a really good thing. But I need Your help to unwrap this gift. Reveal to me who the Holy Spirit is, what He is like, what He does, and how He works, so I can experience every blessing You mean for Him to be in my life.

Amen.

THE MYSTERIOUS HOLY SPIRIT

God is mysterious in many ways, but one of the most mysterious aspects of His nature is that He is three personalities all rolled into one God. He is God the Father, Jesus the Son, and the Holy Spirit.

The Holy Spirit is sometimes a bit more difficult to relate to than God or Jesus. He seems sort of like a ghost or a force instead of a person. The truth is, though, that the Holy Spirit is the part of God that is closest to you because He lives inside you when you accept God's grace. So who is the Holy Spirit, and what can He mean in your life?

As a graduate with new challenges ahead of you, you need the Holy Spirit's presence in your life now more than ever. God's Spirit gives you a link to His power so that you can live your life with strength and passion. The Holy Spirit is called your Counselor and Comforter, giving you guidance and care no matter what you're facing.

The Holy Spirit is also called the Spirit of Truth. He speaks God's truth to your heart and helps you understand His Word. He is also the giver of spiritual gifts that allow you to fulfill God's special purpose for your life.

God's Holy Spirit is also referred to as a gift. He assures us of God's love and marks us with a seal that guarantees us life forever with God. The Holy Spirit is our closest friend and intimate guide—He will give us the power, strength, joy, and encouragement we need to live our lives for Him.

My Precious Child:

The most profound thing about the Holy Spirit is that He lives inside you. I have always lived alongside My children, but now I actually set up housekeeping in your heart! It is through Him that you and I are made one!

Think of the Holy Spirit as the ultimate Helper, who empowers you to live your very best life. He is exactly what you need when you don't even know what you need. It is through Him that you connect to My power, wisdom, guidance, and comfort. It is through Him that you cultivate a heart more like Mine.

Rely on the Holy Spirit for everything. As you learn to recognize His leading—which you will do through practice—you will find the grace you need in every situation. He is My gift to you to help you fulfill every dream of success.

Your loving Father

Hope

Be strong and take courage,
all you who put your hope in the LORD!
PSALM 31:24 NLT

The hope of the righteous ends in gladness.
PROVERBS 10:28 RSV

The LORD is good to those whose hope is in him,
to the one who seeks him.
LAMENTATIONS 3:25

May the God of hope fill you with all joy and peace in believing, so
that by the power of the Holy Spirit you may abound in hope.
ROMANS 15:13 RSV

The LORD looks after those who fear him,
those who put their hope in his love.
He saves them from death
and spares their lives in times of hunger.
PSALM 33:18-19 NCV

GOD'S GIFT OF HOPE

Congratulations! You have finished a long pursuit of knowledge and are embarking on the next chapter of your life. It's a time for you to celebrate and to look to the future. And God wants to help you celebrate by giving you the awesome gift of His hope. His Word is full of promises about the hope that can be yours as you walk with Him.

God wants to give you hope in His protection. He promises to guard you as you face the uncertainties and dangers of life. He commands His angels to keep watch over you and to defend you against evil.

God also gives you hope through His unfailing love. He will always be with you and love you unconditionally, no matter what. When you struggle with rejection or loneliness, you can be certain that your Heavenly Father will never leave you and will love you forever.

When you are tired and feel like giving up, God gives you hope through His abundant strength. He will always be there beside you to restore you, even in the darkest and most difficult times. Whenever you feel overwhelmed, turn to Him and He promises to give you new strength.

Through all of these gifts, God wants to inspire you with hope for your future. He has incredible plans for you—plans that will surpass your biggest dreams. And if you will only trust in His Son, Jesus, you will also receive the greatest gift of hope—the hope that one day God will bring you home to live with Him forever.

Identity

The apostle Paul said, "I have been crucified with Christ;
and it is no longer I who live, but Christ lives in me; and the life
which I now live in the flesh I live by faith in the Son of God,
who loved me and gave Himself up for me."

GALATIANS 2:20 NASB

We are God's fellow workers; you are God's field, God's building.

1 CORINTHIANS 3:9

Jesus said, "You didn't choose me! I chose you!
I appointed you to go and produce lovely fruit always."

JOHN 15:16 TLB

Jesus said, "You are the light that gives light to the world. . . .
Live so that they will see the good things you do and
will praise your Father in heaven."

MATTHEW 5:14,16 NCV

You are a people set apart as holy to GOD, your God. GOD,
your God, chose you out of all the people on Earth for himself as a
cherished, personal treasure.

DEUTERONOMY 7:6 MSG

You are a chosen people, a royal priesthood,
a holy nation, a people belonging to God.

1 PETER 2:9

WHO AM I?

Now that you're a graduate, you are beginning to find a new identity. This is an exciting time in your life, but it can also leave you confused about who you really are. As you seek out your true identity and your place in the world, God wants to show you who you are in His eyes. Ultimately, God's view of you is the only one that truly matters. The identity you find in Him is the only one that will last forever. So who does God say you are?

First of all, you are God's child. He created you in His own image with your own unique personality, gifts, and talents. He loves you unconditionally, without measure, and wants only the best for you. As His child, you are the heir to all the riches of God's kingdom!

You are also a part of God's team—created to fulfill a specific purpose in His ultimate plan. In the Bible, God calls you His ambassador and His fellow worker. He has given you the all-important task of spreading the message of His love and forgiveness to your part of the world.

And because God lives within you, when you accept His forgiveness, you are His temple, His home. You are considered perfect and holy in His sight because His Spirit fills you.

So as you begin life as a graduate, with new identities and roles to play, remember the incredible identity you have in God's eyes. No matter what changes in your life, you will always be treasured in the eyes of your Father.

Independence

But he's already made it plain how to live, what to do,
what God is looking for in men and women.
It's quite simple: Do what is fair and just to your neighbor,
be compassionate and loyal in your love,
And don't take yourself too seriously—take God seriously.

MICAH 6:8 MSG

The way God designed our bodies is a model for understanding
our lives together as a church: every part dependent on every other
part, the parts we mention and the parts we don't, the parts
we see and the parts we don't. If one part hurts, every other part is
involved in the hurt, and in the healing. If one part flourishes,
every other part enters into the exuberance.

1 CORINTHIANS 12:25-26 MSG

You, brethren, have been called to liberty; only do not use liberty as
an opportunity for the flesh, but through love serve one another.
For all the law is fulfilled in one word, even in this:
"You shall love your neighbor as yourself."

GALATIANS 5:13-14 NKJV

Walk in a manner worthy of the calling with which you have been
called, with all humility and gentleness, with patience,
showing tolerance for one another in love.

EPHESIANS 4:1-2 NASB

Heavenly Father:

Becoming an independent adult—no longer having to answer to my parents for my every action—is exciting. Now I can do what I want to, when I want to do it, as long as it doesn't break the law. It's almost too good to be true!

While I am having a lot of fun, I'm also realizing that my life is now my responsibility. No one is going to make me eat right or get enough sleep. With my own checking account and a job, I am free to spend my money however I want, but it could easily get out of hand.

I need Your help, Father, to keep myself in check. Help me to use my freedom wisely. I may not have to answer to my parents like I used to, but I'll always have to answer to You.

Amen.

THE TRUE MEANING OF INDEPENDENCE

America's Founding Fathers composed our Declaration of Independence upon two fundamental principles: respect for the equality of all people and respect for all people's rights.

Independence, then, is not simply a matter of autonomy, self-sufficiency, and license. It is a matter of dignifying others and practicing a selfless regard for their needs. That is the reason America stands head and shoulders above other nations when it comes to compassion and concern for the welfare of other people. The point is that your independence is only as legitimate as your effectiveness in helping others realize their freedom and happiness.

Now that you're on your own and establishing your independence, consider what the ancient prophet Micah had to say about your responsibility to God and people:

- Act justly. In other words, do what is right regardless. When the culture, the media, and the people around you make an attempt on your integrity, stand firm for what is right, honorable, and respectable.
- Love mercy. Let your first impulse be compassion. The mercy of God is radical, lavish, and costly. Be radically committed to a lavish kind of love, and be ready to make sacrifices.
- Walk humbly with your God. Live in such a way that others can sense your regard for Him—and for them. Champion those who are in need of rescue, mend the brokenhearted, and put the interests of others above your own.

The conclusion of the Declaration pretty well sums it up, for it is as compelling as the preamble: "We mutually pledge to each other our Lives, our Fortunes and our sacred Honor."

My Precious Child:

This is a very exciting time in your life, a season to explore new things and exercise your newfound freedom. But this isn't a license to become self-centered or run wild. With great freedom comes great responsibility.

In many ways you can now do what you want to, but keep in mind that not everything is a good idea. Ask yourself, Will acting on this idea bless others? Will it cause me to grow and become a better person? Concentrate on doing those things that produce good fruit—in either your life or the lives of others.

Your time is now your own. Use it wisely, and I will use you to be a great blessing to others. The world will be a better place because of you.

Your loving Father

Integrity

You are to live clean, innocent lives as children of God
in a dark world full of people who are crooked and stubborn.
Shine out among them like beacon lights, holding out to them
the Word of Life.

PHILIPPIANS 2:15-16 TLB

You have upheld me because of my integrity,
and set me in your presence forever.

PSALM 41:12 NRSV

As for me, I walk in my integrity.

PSALM 26:11 NRSV

Whoever walks in integrity walks securely.

PROVERBS 10:9 NRSV

I will be careful to live a blameless life—
. . .I will lead a life of integrity
in my own home.

PSALM 101:2 NLT

One who walks in integrity will be safe.

PROVERBS 28:18 NRSV

ASK, SEEK, AND KNOCK

To have integrity means to be the same person on the inside that you appear to be on the outside. It holds forth the idea of having integration of thought, character, words, and action. In other words, what you see is what you get.

There is a proven method for establishing that kind of integrity: ask, seek, and knock.

Ask yourself, What do I believe? Examine the principles that govern your life. Some are derived from your upbringing. Others might have developed from those outside your family who have contributed to your life in some meaningful way. Still others spring from inspiring things you have read about people from the past and present. But the most critical source of belief comes from the Word of God. Ask God what to believe in.

Seek a firm commitment with which to back up your belief system. Explore the reasons for your beliefs, and imagine what you would do if they were put to the test. Which of them are you willing to suffer for? die for? Concerning which are you most vulnerable or weakest? Most important, seek God's reinforcements concerning your beliefs.

Knock at the door of opportunity by actively pursuing those principles. In other words, walk the talk. Find ways to demonstrate your integrity on behalf of other people, your community, and your country. And above all things, walk with God through those opportunities, trusting Him to be your strength and resource.

Be a person of integrity. The result will be an extraordinary life that honors God and makes a difference.

Jesus

God, who is rich in mercy, because of His great love with which
He loved us, even when we were dead in trespasses,
made us alive together with Christ (by grace you have been saved),
and raised us up together, and made us sit together
in the heavenly places in Christ Jesus.

EPHESIANS 2:4-6 NKJV

God raised the Lord Jesus from the dead, and we know that God
will also raise us with Jesus. God will bring us together with you,
and we will stand before him.

2 CORINTHIANS 4:14 NCV

Jesus Christ rescued us from this evil world we're in by offering
himself as a sacrifice for our sins.

GALATIANS 1:4 MSG

Now we rejoice in our wonderful new relationship with God—
all because of what our Lord Jesus Christ has done in dying for our
sins—making us friends of God.

ROMANS 5:11 TLB

In [God's] great mercy he has given us new birth into a living hope
through the resurrection of Jesus Christ from the dead.

1 PETER 1:3

GRADUATION TO GLORY

Did you know that Jesus was a graduate too? But His graduation was quite different from yours. There was no robe and no tassel. There was no parade of graduating seniors and no pomp and circumstance. In fact, there was no diploma and certainly no applause.

Jesus was stripped of His meager clothing, then adorned with a purple garment intended to make a mockery of Him. In place of tassels, He wore a crown of thorns that pierced a bloody, sweat-streaked brow. He was paraded, all right—up the Via Dolorosa to Calvary's barren hillside with a crossbeam slung over His bruised shoulders. Once there, He was impaled on a Roman cross, a form of execution reserved for the vilest criminals.

Instead of a diploma, there was a sign posted above His head that published in three different languages the charges brought against Him. And the only applause came from those who jeered at Him, cheering as He suffered and finally expired.

But make no mistake, He did graduate.

Not many days after the crucifixion, the resurrected Jesus rose up from the earth's surface and ascended into the heavens—exalted to the throne of God.

As you graduate, consider Jesus.

It is in possessing true humility that you will find your loftiest experiences. It is in loving unconditionally that you will experience the greatest joy. It is in giving your life for the sake of others that you will find yourself in the end in the very presence of the Almighty.

There is a graduation even grander than that which you have encountered. It is a graduation to glory!

Joy

Let us fix our eyes on Jesus, the author and perfecter of our faith,
who for the joy set before him endured the cross.

HEBREWS 12:2

You have not seen Christ, but still you love him. You cannot see
him now, but you believe in him. So you are filled with a joy that
cannot be explained, a joy full of glory.

1 PETER 1:8 NCV

If we are living in the light of God's presence, just as Christ does,
then we have wonderful fellowship and joy with each other.

1 JOHN 1:7 TLB

You have endowed him with eternal happiness.
You have given him the unquenchable joy of your presence.

PSALM 21:6 TLB

I have indeed received much joy and encouragement
from your love, because the hearts of the saints
have been refreshed through you.

PHILEMON 1:7 NRSV

Salvation comes from God. What joys he gives to all his people.

PSALM 3:8 TLB

Heavenly Father:

I have so much to be thankful for, so much to be happy about, but often I feel empty inside. When I achieve a goal, buy a trendy new outfit or the latest electronic gadget, there's always a thrill at first. But after a while, the newness wears off and the emptiness returns. Then I look to the next new thing that promises to make me more attractive, give me an edge in life, or make me happy, and the cycle begins again. It seems like the whole world is chasing after the pot of gold at the end of the rainbow, only to find out that it is merely an illusion.

There has to be more to life than this, but I need Your help to see it. Show me what real joy is and how to obtain it.

Amen.

THE JOY SET BEFORE YOU

The various stages of life offer different types of joy. When you were an infant, you found great joy in crawling, standing, walking, and climbing. As a young child, you derived great joy from learning how to ride a bike, swimming, hitting a baseball, and water skiing. As you grew older, you became overjoyed at driving solo in the family car, having friends beyond the family circle, and making decisions about where to go and what to do.

Now, as you graduate, you will find yet another kind of joy. Whether it is learning how to function in your job, buying a new house, handling your finances successfully, or diapering your first baby, the delight will always be present.

Though there is a great sense of fulfillment in all that you accomplish in life, the greatest joy of all is found in relationships. From the moment in infancy when you learned your mother's face to the ecstasy you will experience at the sight of your first grandchild, the joy found in people is by far the greatest.

In fact, relationships—and the joy they bring—are the only things you can take into eternity. You can't take your money with you when you die. You certainly can't smuggle your house, your car, your fishing pole, or your wardrobe over the threshold of heaven. But relationships with your friends and family will last forever, both in this life and the one to come.

Jesus knew this to be true. For the joy set before Him—in other words, on behalf of those who would spend eternity with Him—He endured the cross.

Don't miss the joy. Invest yourself in others.

My Precious Child:

Material things and achieving success are blessings from Me, but they were never meant to produce lasting joy. They are temporal pleasures that enrich your life on earth, but you can't take them into eternity.

On the other hand, real and lasting joy comes from relationships—first through a relationship with Me and then through relationships with others. Unlike achievements and material things, relationships are eternal in nature.

Making time for others is a great place to start. Offer a helping hand or lend an open ear to the people in your world. Through reaching out to others by offering a smile, sharing a laugh, or performing an act of kindness, you will in turn reap a joy that far exceeds your investment— and that joy is eternal.

Your loving Father

Knowing God

Jesus said, "This is eternal life: [it means] to know (to perceive, recognize, become acquainted with, and understand) You, the only true and real God, and [likewise] to know Him, Jesus [as the] Christ (the Anointed One, the Messiah), Whom You have sent."

JOHN 17:3 AMP

We have not ceased to pray for you and to ask that you may be filled with the knowledge of His will in all spiritual wisdom and understanding, so that you will walk in a manner worthy of the Lord, to please Him in all respects, bearing fruit in every good work and increasing in the knowledge of God.

COLOSSIANS 1:9-10 NASB

In the past you did not know God. You were slaves to gods that were not real. But now you know the true God. Really, it is God who knows you.

GALATIANS 4:8-9 NCV

I want to know Christ and the power of his resurrection and the fellowship of sharing in his sufferings, becoming like him in his death, and so, somehow, to attain to the resurrection from the dead.

PHILIPPIANS 3:10-11

By this we may be sure that we know him, if we keep his commandments.

1 JOHN 2:3 RSV

WHAT DO YOU KNOW?

A list of things you should know by now:
- how to ride a bike
- how to floss
- how many players make up a baseball team
- how much it costs to get a haircut
- how much to tip the waitstaff

A list of things you will know shortly (if you don't already):
- how to stretch a paycheck to the end of the week
- how to figure your income tax (or find someone who can)
- how to diaper a baby
- how to change a tire
- when to cut down on carbohydrates
- how to do laundry

There are so many demands, so much to know. And in this age of information, knowledge abounds, bombarding us from all directions. Someone has said that today's adult has a very broad spectrum of knowledge, but very little expertise. In other words, you might know about a lot of things, although it might be very little about each. While knowledge is vital, be mindful not to spend all of your energy simply learning facts, figures, and data.

The most profound and fulfilling knowledge you can possibly pursue is a knowledge of God. Knowing God requires a concentrated attempt—it must be intentional. But the time spent is well worth it. Jesus said knowing God leads to everlasting life!

You know a lot now, and you'll learn even more with each passing year. But be sure to invest in the knowledge that will yield the most fulfilling dividends—knowing God, knowing God's people, and knowing God's will for your life.

Learning

Jesus said, "The one who comes to Me
I will certainly not cast out."
JOHN 6:37 NASB

Christ accepted you, so you should accept each other,
which will bring glory to God.
ROMANS 15:7 NCV

He made us accepted in the Beloved.
EPHESIANS 1:6 NKJV

Jesus said, "Whenever a village won't accept you or listen to you,
shake off the dust from your feet as you leave."
MARK 6:11 TLB

If you want favor with both God and man,
and a reputation for good judgment and common sense,
then trust the Lord completely.
PROVERBS 3:4-5 TLB

You bless the righteous, O LORD;
you cover them with favor as with a shield.
PSALM 5:12 NRSV

THE NEVER-ENDING EDUCATION

Just when you thought the learning was over . . .

Here you are, graduated, standing at a significant cross-roads in life. Looking behind, you realize how far you've come and how much knowledge you've acquired to this point. It is mind-boggling. Looking ahead, you will find continuing education related to your job, family life, finances, government, and community. It is staggering to consider the learning that is yet before you.

You'll find communication skills on that list as well: how to listen better, how to speak more effectively, and how to write more proficiently. Your abilities will improve through use over time.

In addition, you will continue to improve your reading skills: you'll read at a faster rate of speed; you'll find your comprehension increasing; you'll be more capable of discernment and independent thought. Your reasoning abilities will be more thorough, and you'll have more to contribute to conversations.

While you are at it, why not try out some of those reading skills on the Scriptures. Spend some time every day in the Word of God, learning what is on the Lord's mind and discovering what He holds dear to His heart.

Then exercise your communication skills on Him. Begin and end your day in prayer, whether by writing in a journal or verbally opening your heart to Him. Speak to Him concerning the affairs of your existence, and listen to Him concerning the affairs of His kingdom.

For those who mean to live life to the full—enjoying everything that is available to them—the learning will never stop. The more you know, the deeper you'll go! Never, never stop learning.

Loneliness

Turn to me and be gracious to me,
For I am lonely and afflicted.
The troubles of my heart are enlarged;
Bring me out of my distresses.

PSALM 25:16-17 NASB

God is in his holy Temple.
He is a father to orphans,
and he defends the widows.
God gives the lonely a home.

PSALM 68:5-6 NCV

Jesus said, "If you love me, obey me; and I will ask the Father and
he will give you another Comforter, and he will never leave you."

JOHN 14:15-16 TLB

Jesus said, "I am with you always, to the close of the age."

MATTHEW 28:20 RSV

May your unfailing love be my comfort,
according to your promise to your servant.

PSALM 119:76

Heavenly Father:

So much has changed, including many of my relationships. Many who have been part of my everyday life aren't there anymore, and I feel lonely and even a little afraid. I don't want to feel sorry for myself, but this is painful; and I don't know what to do to change it. I feel like I'm walking a deserted path in the wilderness that no one else has traveled.

I'm hoping that this loneliness won't last long, but while I'm in this season, help me to discover what I need to know about myself and why I am here on earth. I also want to know You better. Help me to take advantage of this time and get the most out of it.

Then, when the time is right, I trust You to bring new relationships into my life—relationships where You are at the center.

Amen.

FORGED IN THE DESERT

His was a lonely life. John the Baptist received direction from God indicating that his mission was to be fulfilled in the wilderness. Instead of being called to the religious center of activity, he was sent away. His message was a herald of warning, a radical plea for repentance, a confrontation with ungodly people in ungodly situations.

John's attire and eating habits were a bit eccentric. That set him apart from his contemporaries even more. He dressed in a hairy garment tied with a crude leather belt. He ate locusts and wild honey. People had a difficult time relating to his extreme lifestyle. But John was faithful to his God, and a multitude of people responded to his message.

John's conviction brought him into conflict with a ruler plagued with an inflated ego. The ruler put John in prison for speaking out against his adulterous marriage and later had John killed.

John's was a lonely life. However, he turned his loneliness into a great witness for the Lord. John used the solitude to study his God. He disciplined his emotions and kept himself under the Spirit's reign. John spent his energies on executing his mission, not on feeling sorry for himself. He was a courageous champion for the cause of Christ.

If now, with school behind you, you find yourself lonely for a while, don't despair. There are things learned in the wilderness that can deepen your understanding of why you are here, help you discover your purpose, and forge your faith for completing your mission. Learn what you can during this season; your future will be richer for it.

My Precious Child:

You are at a new place in your life. Times of solitude can lead to great discoveries about who I've called you to be and where you're going. Only when you are stretched beyond what you think you are capable of will you discover the power and strength within you.

It's tough to be alone, but Jesus understands it. He was utterly alone as He hung on the cross and I had to turn away from Him. It was the deepest loneliness anyone has ever experienced, but He did it for you. Now you never have to be alone again. I am always with you and will never leave or forsake you. People will come and go out of your life, but I am here to stay.

Your loving Father

Love

Love endures long and is patient and kind; love never is envious nor boils over with jealousy, is not boastful or vainglorious, does not display itself haughtily. It is not conceited (arrogant and inflated with pride); it is not rude (unmannerly) and does not act unbecomingly. Love (God's love in us) does not insist on its own rights or its own way, for it is not self-seeking; it is not touchy or fretful or resentful; it takes no account of the evil done to it [it pays no attention to a suffered wrong]. It does not rejoice at injustice and unrighteousness, but rejoices when right and truth prevail. Love bears up under anything and everything that comes, is ever ready to believe the best of every person, its hopes are fadeless under all circumstances, and it endures everything [without weakening]. Love never fails [never fades out or becomes obsolete or comes to an end].

1 CORINTHIANS 13:4-8 AMP

God has poured out his love into our hearts by the Holy Spirit, whom he has given us.

ROMANS 5:5

God is love, and all who live in love live in God, and God lives in them. And as we live in God, our love grows more perfect.

1 JOHN 4:16-17 NLT

Jesus said, "You have heard that it was said, 'You shall love your neighbor and hate your enemy.' But I say to you, love your enemies."

MATTHEW 5:43-44 NKJV

WHAT IS LOVE, ANYWAY?

Love is a word that is greatly overused and misunderstood. If you say that you love God, you don't mean that you love Him like you love pizza, do you? Of course not.

The Greek language is far more specific in describing the various forms of love. *Eros* is used to describe sexual love. *Phileo* is used of the brotherly love that one has for friends and acquaintances. *Storge* is the affectionate love that a grandparent has for a grandchild.

But *agape*, or God's love, is by far the most powerful and far-reaching. In fact, God is *agape*. It is the self-sacrificing, unconditional love that He has for all people, the love that motivated Jesus to suffer on the cross to purchase your salvation. It is the love that refuses to give up on you, that always believes the best about you. It is the love that transforms you and never fails.

When you become a believer in Christ, that love comes to live in your heart, and you are then capable of loving people the way God does. Sound impossible? What about those who mistreat you, those you don't even like? That is one of the things that makes God's love so amazing. While the other types of love are based upon feelings, *agape* is simply a choice, a decision to love because every person is priceless in God's eyes.

As you enter this new phase of your life, you want to have a positive impact and make a difference. By allowing God to love others through you, you will find that love changing your world, one person at a time.

Loving Others

Jesus said, "When you give a luncheon or a dinner, do not invite your friends or your brothers or your relatives or rich neighbors, otherwise they may also invite you in return and that will be your repayment. But when you give a reception, invite the poor, the crippled, the lame, the blind, and you will be blessed, since they do not have the means to repay you; for you will be repaid at the resurrection of the righteous."

LUKE 14:12-14 NASB

Peter addressed them, "You know, I'm sure that this is highly irregular. Jews just don't do this—visit and relax with people of another race. But God has just shown me that no race is better than any other."

ACTS 10:28 MSG

Jesus said, "Love your enemies. Do good to those who hate you. Pray for the happiness of those who curse you. Pray for those who hurt you. . . . Do you think you deserve credit merely for loving those who love you? Even the sinners do that! And if you do good only to those who do good to you, is that so wonderful? Even sinners do that much! . . . Love your enemies! Do good to them! Lend to them! And don't be concerned that they might not repay. Then your reward from heaven will be very great, and you will truly be acting as children of the Most High, for he is kind to the unthankful and to those who are wicked. You must be compassionate, just as your Father is compassionate."

LUKE 6:27-28,32-33,35-36 NLT

LOVING DIFFERENCES

It isn't difficult to love people who are just like you. The tough part is loving people who aren't.

Jesus' popularity was at an all-time high. People were carried away with His teaching, His healing miracles, and His power to provide. He couldn't go anywhere in public without a mob following.

"John, we'll be leaving early in the morning for Tyre," Peter said.

"Tyre? It's full of heathens," John argued.

"All the more reason the multitude won't follow," Peter assured him. "But the Lord has a friend there—he's one of us."

Upon arrival, the Lord slipped into the house secretly, but a woman ran through the doorway immediately and collapsed at His feet.

"Sir, I've heard about You—that You even have authority over demons. Could You please come heal my daughter who is possessed by evil spirits?" she begged.

Jesus spoke to her gently, "First I should help my own family, the Jews. It isn't right to take food from the children and throw it to the dogs."

She replied, "That's true, Lord, but even the dogs under the table are given some crumbs from the children's plates."

"Good answer!" Jesus grinned with delight. This foreigner believed that Jesus had the power to heal, and she understood His mission to love. "And because you have answered so well, I have healed your daughter." (See Mark 7:24-30 NLT).

Cultivate a willingness to love others, even those who are not like you.

Money

If we have enough food and clothing, let us be content. But people who long to be rich fall into temptation and are trapped by many foolish and harmful desires that plunge them into ruin and destruction. For the love of money is at the root of all kinds of evil. And some people, craving money, have wandered from the faith and pierced themselves with many sorrows.

1 TIMOTHY 6:8-10 NLT

Jesus said, "Don't worry and say, 'What will we eat?' or 'What will we drink?' or 'What will we wear?' The people who don't know God keep trying to get these things, and your Father in heaven knows you need them. The thing you should want most is God's kingdom and doing what God wants. Then all these other things you need will be given to you."

MATTHEW 6:31-33 NCV

You can be sure that God will take care of everything you need, his generosity exceeding even yours in the glory that pours from Jesus.

PHILIPPIANS 4:19 MSG

Jesus said, "The worries of the world, and the deceitfulness of riches, and the desires for other things enter in and choke the word, and it becomes unfruitful."

MARK 4:19 NASB

Heavenly Father:

I want to have the right attitude about money, and I don't want to spend my life worrying about it or striving to obtain more than I should. I want to view it from Your perspective.

But I have so many questions. How much should I save? How much do You want me to give to Your work? How much can I spend on myself? I need Your help to establish a workable budget; then I'll need Your grace to stick to it. Strengthen me with self-control so I won't over-spend, but also remind me to be generous when I try to hang on too tightly.

As I grow in my ability to handle money, I pray that You will bring promotions so I'll have the opportunity to manage more. Help me to keep all of this in proper perspective so that all my financial dealings honor You.

Amen.

THE MAIN THING—NOT MONEY

"Dad, I need to find a job that will pay a decent salary right off," Ted said after graduating from college.

"What do you consider decent?" Butch replied.

"Enough to afford a mortgage, two car payments, and eventually to start a family."

"When your mother and I married, we started a family, then got a job, shared a car, and rented a small duplex for a while. It was seven years before we finally bought a house."

"Seven years!" Ted was aghast. "We can't wait seven years! We'll blow all our money on rent."

"What makes you think that's 'blowing' money?"

"You've got to invest your money these days, Dad."

"You've got to invest yourself, son—your time, talents, and treasures. In spite of what our culture suggests, money is not the most important thing."

"Are you suggesting that Missy and I shouldn't be concerned about investments?" Ted pressed.

"I'm saying that you and Missy should be concerned about having integrity, learning how to share with people in need, and having the family you've dreamed of."

"Your way of thinking is just obsolete. Money is a bigger issue today than it was in your day, Dad."

"Wow, I wish someone had told me that before. . . ."

"Before what?"

"Your mother and I could have had a mortgage and a couple of cars instead of you!"

Starting out, many think that making money should be the first priority. Money is essential. However, money is not the first essential. Keep it in perspective.

My Precious Child:

Money is a very important and complex issue. That's why I talk about it so much in My Word. Financial abundance comes from Me, but great wisdom is needed to handle it properly. Money is a powerful tool for good, and it is necessary to function in this world—but it can also be very dangerous if it isn't handled properly.

Maintain a healthy attitude about money by always being grateful for what you have. I want My people to enjoy life and have money left over to give to others, but I don't want it to be the main focus.

Live with an open hand, willing to freely distribute to others. This is an attitude that I can bless, and I will see to it that you have everything you need—and more.

Your loving Father

Parents

"Honor your father and mother"—which is the first commandment
with a promise—"that it may go well with you and that you
may enjoy long life on the earth."

EPHESIANS 6:2-3

Each of you must respect his mother and father,
and you must observe my Sabbaths. I am the LORD your God.

LEVITICUS 19:3

You created my inmost being;
you knit me together in my mother's womb.

PSALM 139:13

Hear, my child, your father's instruction,
and do not reject your mother's teaching.

PROVERBS 1:8 NRSV

Listen to your father, who gave you life,
and do not despise your mother when she is old.

PROVERBS 23:22

Love one another with mutual affection;
outdo one another in showing honor.

ROMANS 12:10 NRSV

LOVE WELL, LIVE LONG

The fifth commandment states: "'Honor your father and your mother, so that you may live long" (Exodus 20:12). It is the only command that has a promise attached.

"What does it mean exactly?" you ask.

The answer: It means exactly what it says—no contingencies, no exceptions.

Look at it from every angle and watch it become doable.

- Honor your parents for who they have been in the past. You don't have to agree with your parents' child-rearing techniques to honor them. The fact is, they gave you life, nurtured you, provided a home, and did their best to equip you for life. If your parents dropped the ball in any of these areas, you can redeem a great deal of the past by honoring them anyway.

- Honor your parents for who they are in the present. Some graduates are surrounded with a network of support. Others feel, more or less, on their own. Either way, the most promising thing you can do for the current state of your relationship is to treat your parents the way you want to be treated. Give them your respect, not simply because they deserve it, but because it is within you to do so.

- Honor your parents for who they will be in the future. If you are committed to treating your parents honorably, you can bet that they will become better people for it. The higher your esteem, the higher they will reach.

The reason for this commandment is obvious: It is good for everyone. Whether you think your parents deserve honor or not, you will be a more honorable person for extending it to them.

Passion

God wants you to be holy and pure, and to keep clear of
all sexual sin so that each of you will marry in holiness and honor—
not in lustful passion as the heathen do, in their
ignorance of God and his ways.

1 THESSALONIANS 4:3-5 TLB

Shun youthful passions and pursue righteousness, faith, love, and
peace, along with those who call on the Lord from a pure heart.

2 TIMOTHY 2:22 NRSV

Wait passionately for GOD,
don't leave the path.

PSALM 37:34 MSG

Do not let sin exercise dominion in your mortal bodies, to make
you obey their passions. No longer present your members to sin as
instruments of wickedness, but present yourselves to God as those
who have been brought from death to life, and present your
members to God as instruments of righteousness.

ROMANS 6:12-13 NRSV

Those who belong to Christ Jesus have crucified the flesh
with its passions and desires.

GALATIANS 5:24 NRSV

THE BAROMETER OF THE SOUL

"Why didn't you go to battle with your men?" Kemuel asked.

"I'm restless—weary of bloodshed," King David answered.

"But your men look to you for strength and courage. They need you," the aide argued.

"I'm the king, Kemuel. I don't have to fight anymore, I simply command the army. Anyway, I'm going to bed." At that, David turned into his chamber and disrobed.

Sleep wouldn't come. David lay awake, staring into the night. There was a peculiar emptiness inside him lately. He remembered earlier times when his energies were spent tending sheep, protecting them from lions and bears. He remembered the days of exile before he assumed the throne. He thrived on the challenge of leading the ragamuffins who eventually became great heroes of Israel—the mighty men.

He walked out onto the roof to sit under the stars.

"What's this?" His eyes caught sight of a phantom of beauty. A woman was bathing in the moonlight on her own rooftop.

"Kemuel," David rushed into his aide's chamber. "There is a woman on her rooftop. Go get her for me."

"Sir, isn't that Bathsheba? The wife of one of your mighty men?"

"You heard me," David ordered.

The heady effects of power had caused King David to no longer feel accountable to his people. His passions misfired, and instead of panting after God, he spent himself on his lust, imposing devastating consequences upon his family and his future. (See 2 Samuel 11.)

Your passions are a true barometer of your soul. Pay attention to what they are telling you.

Peace

Don't worry about anything; instead, pray about everything;
tell God your needs and don't forget to thank him for his answers.
If you do this you will experience God's peace, which is far more
wonderful than the human mind can understand.
His peace will keep your thoughts and your hearts quiet
and at rest as you trust in Christ Jesus.

PHILIPPIANS 4:6-7 TLB

Peace I leave with you; My [own] peace I now give and bequeath to
you. Not as the world gives do I give to you. Do not let your hearts
be troubled, neither let them be afraid. [Stop allowing yourselves to
be agitated and disturbed; and do not permit yourselves to be
fearful and intimidated and cowardly and unsettled.]

JOHN 14:27 AMP

I lay down and slept in peace and woke up safely,
for the Lord was watching over me.

PSALM 3:5 TLB

Wisdom gives:
A long, good life, riches, honor, pleasure, peace.

PROVERBS 3:16-17 TLB

I pray that God our Father and the Lord Jesus Christ
will give each of you his fullest blessings, and his peace in
your hearts and your lives.

PHILIPPIANS 1:2 TLB

Heavenly Father:

Even though I am Your child, I am not exempt from the storms of life. I realize that there will always be challenges, but through each one I want to learn more about myself, my relationship with You, and the truth of Your Word.

Help me not to be seized with alarm when troubles arise, but lead me to scriptures that will encourage my faith and settle my heart. Help me not to put You in a box by expecting You to resolve situations the way I think You should. Remind me that You are utterly trustworthy and that I can trust You to work things out for my good.

I want to always rest in the peace that Jesus promised, that peace that passes anything my mind can comprehend.

Amen.

PEACE THAT PASSES UNDERSTANDING

The twelve men felt pretty confident as they got into the boat that evening. Four of them were fishermen, having logged many hours at sea. Besides, there were other boats setting sail alongside.

Jesus found a spot in the stern and, weary from the day's activity, reclined to rest. Pillowing His head on a cushion, He fell fast asleep.

"James, do you see that angry cloud sweeping in from the west?" John stood frowning at the sky.

"Surely it isn't a squall swooping in through the gorge." James winced at the darkening sky.

"I'm afraid it is. I hear the wind howling through the pass," John continued. "Maybe we'll make the shore before she blows."

Minutes later, waves were lashing at the boat and breaking over the deck.

"Master, wake up!" Peter shouted. "Don't You care that we are about to drown?"

Jesus sat up from His sleep. He stood into the wind, and just as a wave rose up and pitched itself against the small ship, Jesus said sternly, "Quiet! Be still!"

Instantly, all was calm. No wind. No waves. No storm. The sullen sky retreated, brooding over the sudden rebuke.

It wasn't what the twelve were expecting. He frightened them with His power over the elements. (See Mark 4:35-41.)

Now that you are grown and facing life on your own, you should know that even with Jesus in your ship, storms will come. Furthermore, the peace that God brings into a situation will not always be what you anticipate. Be prepared—for sometimes heaven's peace is a peace so astonishing, it passes understanding.

My Precious Child:

Unfortunately, life on earth does come with challenges. I never promised that you would be exempt from them, but I did promise never to leave you without aid or support. In the midst of the storm, never forget that I am there. I am your peace. When you feel the pressure and strain mounting, remember I am indeed working things out for your good. Knowing this and meditating on it will restore peace to your heart and mind.

Don't worry about how I will resolve problems. All you need to know is that you can trust Me and that I am at work. Receive My peace, and let it envelop you. The storm is for only a moment, but My peace will last a lifetime.

Your loving Father

Perseverance

Consider it all joy, my brethren, when you encounter various trials,
knowing that the testing of your faith produces endurance.
And let endurance have its perfect result,
so that you may be perfect and complete, lacking in nothing . . .
Blessed is a man who perseveres under trial;
for once he has been approved, he will receive the crown of life
which the Lord has promised to those who love Him.

JAMES 1:2-4,12 NASB

You need to persevere so that when you have done the will of God,
you will receive what he has promised.

HEBREWS 10:36

In hope we have been saved, but hope that is seen is not hope;
for who hopes for what he already sees? But if we hope for what we
do not see, with perseverance we wait eagerly for it.

ROMANS 8:24-25 NASB

We consider blessed those who have persevered. You have heard of
Job's perseverance and have seen what the Lord finally brought
about. The Lord is full of compassion and mercy.

JAMES 5:11

PERSEVERANCE PAYS OFF

There is an interesting set of algebraic equations for perseverance in the first chapter of James in the Bible. Here is what it says:

Troubles + faith = endurance. Endurance = strength of character. Strength of character = joy. The sum of all is perseverance.

Examine it in separate components for better understanding.

- *Troubles + faith = endurance.* In whatever trial you face, be diligent in your faith. Practice a relentless trust in God—confident of His faithfulness—and pray consistently for wisdom, expecting that He will answer your request. Oddly enough, the disciplines of faith will increase your stamina. You will grow stronger in your relationship with the Lord and gain valuable insight into your circumstances, yourself, and the reason for your struggle.

- *Endurance = strength of character.* As your endurance multiplies, you gain strength of character. You find that your personality and your values are better defined because of the testing you undergo. You are able to deal with life's challenges in a victorious, productive, and God-honoring manner.

- *Strength of character = joy.* In all of this, you learn to "consider it all joy"—so much joy that you welcome the trial. You will find that you are able to praise God for the opportunity to grow stronger, to trust Him more, and to become better equipped for the future.

- *Faith + endurance + strength of character + joy = perseverance.* And perseverance pays off with what the Bible calls "the crown of life."

When you begin to apply these equations to real-life situations, this one will prove to be among the most practical.

Perspective

Jesus said, "What is impossible from a human perspective
is possible with God."
LUKE 18:27 NLT

If you're serious about living this new resurrection life with Christ,
act like it. Pursue the things over which Christ presides.
Don't shuffle along, eyes to the ground, absorbed with the things
right in front of you. Look up, and be alert to what is going on
around Christ—that's where the action is.
See things from his perspective.
COLOSSIANS 3:1-2 MSG

It's important to look at things from God's point of view.
1 CORINTHIANS 4:6 MSG

Why are you down in the dumps, dear soul?
Why are you crying the blues?
Fix my eyes on God—
soon I'll be praising again.
He puts a smile on my face.
He's my God.
PSALM 42:5 MSG

We have the mind of Christ (the Messiah) and do hold the thoughts
(feelings and purposes) of His heart.
1 CORINTHIANS 2:16 AMP

DEVELOPING DOUBLE VISION

There is a little fish, ranging from two to six inches in length, which lives just off the Galapagos Islands, called the *dialommus fuscus*, also known as the four-eyed blenny. The uniqueness of this little fish resides in its peculiar eyesight, for it has the ability to see double.

Granted, for most creatures that wouldn't be an advantage; it would be a liability. In fact, humans spend vast sums of money and go through lots of therapy trying to correct double vision.

So what makes it an asset for the small sea creature? The reason this visual characteristic is so valuable to the *dialommus fuscus* is because it spends its life in shallow tide pools along the coast of Santa Cruz. Lying in the shallow water, the fish can position itself so that the water level hits the middle of its eyes. It can adjust its vision to see under the water and above the water at the same time. And amazingly, its brain is built to process both images to its advantage.

There's a lesson in this quirky member of God's creation. If you practice the ability to discern the higher meaning in situations by looking for God's perspective on the issues, while at the same time interpreting circumstances through the human perspective by keeping in touch with practical matters, you will find yourself at a great advantage. There is a spiritual outlook through which every human event may be perceived. Jesus had that kind of double vision.

As you graduate, broaden your perspective. Take a lesson from a little fish.

Power

I pray that you will begin to understand how incredibly great his power is to help those who believe him. It is that same mighty power that raised Christ from the dead.

EPHESIANS 1:19-20 TLB

I ask you again, does God give you the power of the Holy Spirit and work miracles among you as a result of your trying to obey the Jewish laws? No, of course not. It is when you believe in Christ and fully trust him.

GALATIANS 3:5 TLB

I am not ashamed of the gospel,
for it is the power of God for salvation to everyone who believes.

ROMANS 1:16 NASB

To all who received him, who believed in his name,
he gave power to become children of God.

JOHN 1:12 RSV

Jesus said, "When the Holy Spirit comes to you,
you will receive power."

ACTS 1:8 NCV

We have this treasure in earthen vessels, that the excellence of the power may be of God and not of us.

2 CORINTHIANS 4:7 NKJV

Heavenly Father:

You are an awesome God. I believe You are almighty and that nothing is too difficult for You. When I look around, I see evidence of Your power everywhere—from the vastness of the universe to the meticulous detail with which You fashioned me, from lightning flashing across the sky to a gentle rain shower. Your power is at work all around.

I also see Your power as it is revealed in Your Word. Whether it operated through Jesus or any of the believers, Your power flowed through them, and circumstances changed. Miracles took place.

I need Your power to work in my life. I face impossible situations at times, and You are my only hope. Teach me about Your power and let it flow through me.

Amen.

POWER YOU CANNOT SEE

"Jesus of Nazareth!" The man had a Roman accent.

Jesus turned to see who was calling His name.

"Please come with me! My son is dying!" The man seemed desperate, running toward the Lord. He had run all the way from Capernaum, about twenty-five miles away.

Jesus shook His head sadly and said, "Unless you people see miraculous signs and wonders, you will never believe."

"Sir, come with me before my child dies," the Roman official pleaded once again.

Jesus replied simply, "You may go. Your son will live."

The man took Jesus at His word and headed home. If he believed that Jesus could heal his son if he came to Capernaum, why couldn't He do the same miraculous work from a distance? While en route, the official's servants met him with news that his son had recovered.

"What time did he get better?" the man asked.

After comparing notes with his servants, the man realized that his son was healed at the exact time that Jesus said to him, "Your son will live." (See John 4:46-54.)

Now is the time to realize that God's awesome power is at work, whether you can see it or not. Instead of limiting your thinking to "Seeing is believing," approach situations God's way: "Believe—and then you will see."

My Precious Child:

Wind is an amazing force. You cannot see it with your eyes, but evidence of it is unmistakable. From a gentle breeze to a roaring hurricane, wind makes its presence known. My power is much like the wind. You can't see it either, but there is no denying when it leaves its mark.

Did you know that the power with which I raised Christ from the dead dwells inside all of My children—including you? And it is capable of changing everyone and everything that comes into contact with it.

When you pray, know that My power goes to work to transform the situation you've brought before Me. But be patient and give it time to bring about the desired result. You may not see it immediately, but in time, the evidence of My power will be unmistakable.

Your loving Father

Prayer

Jesus said, "Here's what I want you to do: Find a quiet,
secluded place so you won't be tempted to role-play before God.
Just be there as simply and honestly as you can manage.
The focus will shift from you to God, and you will begin to sense his
grace. The world is full of so-called prayer warriors who are
prayer-ignorant. They're full of formulas and programs and advice,
peddling techniques for getting what you want from God.
Don't fall for that nonsense. This is your Father you are dealing
with, and he knows better than you what you need.
With a God like this loving you, you can pray very simply."

MATTHEW 6:6-9 MSG

Jesus said, "Whatever you ask for in prayer, believe that you have
received it, and it will be yours. And when you stand praying,
if you hold anything against anyone, forgive him, so that your
Father in heaven may forgive you your sins."

MARK 11:24-25

GOD'S Decree . . .
"They'll pray to me by name
and I'll answer them personally."

ZECHARIAH 13:8-9 MSG

Now this is the confidence that we have in Him, that if we ask
anything according to His will, He hears us. And if we know that
He hears us, whatever we ask, we know that we have the petitions
that we have asked of Him.

1 JOHN 5:14-15 NKJV

GOD'S GUIDE TO PRAYER

When you think about prayer, what comes to mind? Does prayer seem to you like something mysterious and only for super-religious types? While prayer's power is mysterious, God does not want the act of prayer to be a mystery to you. Prayer is simply a conversation with Him—like talking with a good friend or a loving parent.

To help you know how to pray, God has given you a model prayer. You probably know it as the Lord's Prayer. When you struggle to know where to begin, you can always pray this prayer straight from the Bible. You can also use it simply as a guide for putting together a prayer in your own words. Here are the parts of God's model prayer:

- It starts out by praising God for who He is and for His good work in our lives and in the world.
- Next, it focuses on our personal needs and asks God to provide for us.
- The third section asks God to forgive us for disobeying Him and to help us forgive others as readily and graciously as He forgives us.
- Next, the prayer asks for God's protection from temptation and evil.
- Finally, it ends with praising Him again.

As you begin life on your own after graduation, prayer can bring you the guidance and comfort you need for whatever you face. Take time to talk with God and to allow Him to speak to you each day. You'll find peace and direction as you make prayer a vital part of your life.

Pressure

Jesus said,
"God blesses those who realize their need for him,
for the Kingdom of Heaven is given to them.
God blesses those who mourn,
for they will be comforted.
God blesses those who are gentle and lowly,
for the whole earth will belong to them.
God blesses those who are hungry and thirsty for justice,
for they will receive it in full.
God blesses those who are merciful,
for they will be shown mercy.
God blesses those whose hearts are pure,
for they will see God.
God blesses those who work for peace,
for they will be called the children of God.
God blesses those who are persecuted because they live for God,
for the Kingdom of Heaven is theirs.
"God blesses you when you are mocked and persecuted and lied
about because you are my followers. Be happy about it! Be very glad!
For a great reward awaits you in heaven. And remember, the
ancient prophets were persecuted, too."

MATTHEW 5:3-12 NLT

RELIEVING THE PRESSURE BY REVERSING THE STANDARD

Now that you've graduated, the pressure is on—pressure to
- establish a career.
- perform well in your job.
- acquire material possessions.
- gain power, position, and influence.
- track an upwardly mobile path.

Right?

Wrong.

Jesus said, "In this world you will have trouble. But take heart! I have overcome the world" (John 16:33).

Knowing God's truth—absolute truth—takes the pressure off. He turns the whole situation inside out. Here's how:

- God rejoices over you when you don't have a superiority complex; for humble people inhabit high places.
- God rejoices when you admit you were wrong, for people learn to trust you.
- God rejoices when you consider others more important than yourself, for people learn to love you.
- God rejoices over you when you seek His will, His way; for you find your efforts more effective.
- God rejoices over you when, instead of demanding a pound of flesh, you give yourself away; for you'll receive mercy in return for mercy.
- God rejoices over those who help establish peace instead of causing conflict, for people find rest in your friendship.

When you feel that the pressure is on, just remember: Jesus relieves the pressure by reversing the standard. When you do the same, you will experience true, lasting, and fulfilling success, and your light will shine as a beacon of hope to others.

Priorities

Jesus said, "Seek first his kingdom and his righteousness,
and all these things will be given to you as well."
MATTHEW 6:33

Jesus said, "You shall love the Lord your God with all your heart,
and with all your soul, and with all your mind. This is the great
and first commandment. And a second is like it,
You shall love your neighbor as yourself."
MATTHEW 22:37-39 RSV

If you really fulfill the royal law according to the Scripture,
"You shall love your neighbor as yourself," you do well.
JAMES 2:8 NKJV

O God, You are my God;
Early will I seek You.
PSALM 63:1 NKJV

I will follow your orders with all my heart.
PSALM 119:69 NCV

Jesus said, "In everything, therefore, treat people the same way you
want them to treat you, for this is the Law and the Prophets."
MATTHEW 7:12 NASB

Heavenly Father:

Sometimes I have so much to do that it is difficult to prioritize. I know time with You should come first, but with all the other commitments I have, something always seems to get in the way. I'm really sorry about that and ask You to forgive me. Show me how to rearrange my schedule so that I can put You first.

I need help with all the other priorities in my life too. I don't see how I can possibly do everything, so help me discern what is really important and which things I can let go. Help me to live a balanced life so I won't burn out, and show me how to get the most out of every minute.

Amen.

WHAT'S MOST IMPORTANT?

Now that you're a graduate, many new demands and commitments are vying for your attention and energy. With a new job, new friends, new financial concerns, and new freedoms, you have a lot on your plate. You know that you need to prioritize these things so you can manage your time and resources and avoid burnout, but how do you know what should be most important?

God placed a simple guide in His Word to help you always know how to set the right priorities in your life. First, He says that the highest priority should be to love Him with your whole being. Building your relationship with God and obeying His words should come before anything else. When you find other activities, or even people, are causing you to neglect time with God, you know that it is time to reorder your priorities.

God says that your second priority should be to love others as you love yourself, to put their interests ahead of your own. If you find yourself making choices that help you get ahead or get what you want at the expense of other people, then you need to rethink your priorities.

As you work to fit in all the aspects of a busy life, remember God's guide to prioritizing. Test your choices—are you putting God first and the interests of others above your own? When you set your priorities according to God's plan, you'll find everything falling into its proper place.

My Precious Child:

I know you have a lot of demands on your time, and I want to help you with all of them. Finding time for Me is not quite as hard as you might think. Try talking to Me when you're in the shower. Sing praises to me while listening to an inspirational CD in your car. Read your Bible on your lunch break. Sit quietly in My presence for a few minutes before you go to sleep at night.

Investing time in your significant human relationships is also important. It is through your love, kind words, and good deeds that others will see My love in action.

Loving Me and loving others are the two most important priorities. As you are faithful to these two things, you will naturally fulfill your responsibilities to Me, your family, friends, job, and church.

Your loving Father

Purity

Even a child is known by his deeds,
Whether what he does is pure and right.

PROVERBS 20:11 NKJV

God, examine me and know my heart. . . .
See if there is any bad thing in me.
Lead me on the road to everlasting life.

PSALM 139:23-24 NCV

Happy are those who live pure lives,
who follow the LORD'S teachings.

PSALM 119:1 NCV

Let no one look down on your youthfulness, but rather in speech,
conduct, love, faith and purity, show yourself an example of those
who believe.

1 TIMOTHY 4:12 NASB

Teach me your ways, O LORD,
that I may live according to your truth!
Grant me purity of heart,
that I may honor you.

PSALM 86:11 NLT

PURE JOY!

One of the qualities that draws us to children is their purity: pure hearts, pure motives, pure language, and pure actions. They are fresh, unsullied specimens of the human race. Their untarnished perspective provides them the coveted freedom to indulge in life without inhibitions or regret. And perhaps the most distinguishable characteristic associated with that kind of purity is unrestrained joy.

Though you are no longer a child, you are in the enviable position of standing at the threshold of a new beginning. It is a perfect opportunity to restore the pure joy of your younger years.

Here are some suggestions:

First, examine your heart on a regular basis. Prayer is one of the most effective ways to keep your motives pure. Allow the gentle light of truth to probe the dark corners of your heart, so nothing takes root within you that will infect your life.

Next, listen to yourself when you talk. Do your words bring out the best in people? Consider whether your conversations build up the reputations of others or tear them down. Replay the tone of your voice and the words you use in order to determine whether they reflect well upon your own character and intentions.

Finally, ask yourself if your actions, habits, and conduct—both public and private—are those that honor God and cause people to respect you. Poor habits are much more difficult to break than they are to avoid in the first place.

Sound difficult? Just remember that the result of your efforts to live a pure life will be purest joy! The more diligence you apply to these matters, the greater the abundance.

Purpose

It is God who works in you to will and
to act according to his good purpose.

PHILIPPIANS 2:13

We know that God causes all things to work together for good
to those who love God, to those who are called according
to His purpose.

ROMANS 8:28 NASB

If you are wise, live a life of steady goodness,
so that only good deeds will pour forth.

JAMES 3:13 TLB

You were called for the very purpose
that you might inherit a blessing.

1 PETER 3:9 NASB

Jesus said, "It is more blessed to give than to receive."

ACTS 20:35 NASB

The one who plants and the one who waters have
a common purpose, and each will receive wages according to
the labor of each. For we are God's servants, working together;
you are God's field, God's building.

1 CORINTHIANS 3:8-9 NRSV

LIVE TO GIVE

When Anne Sullivan Macy accepted the role of governess for the young Helen Keller, she had no idea what the outcome of her efforts would be. After a very trying initiation, she was able to serve as the unselfish catalyst through whom Helen's deliverance from silent darkness came. For nearly fifty years, she was the faithful companion to one of America's foremost humanitarians. Helen's life was an unbelievable triumph on a personal level and an amazing inspiration to all.

Ironically, Anne's great purpose in life was revealed to her very slowly, one day at a time, as she devoted herself to the welfare of another individual. Had she kept to herself, she would never have risen to such heights nor experienced such fulfillment.

Likewise, your true purpose will be most effectively realized through your investment in the lives of others. If you become a teacher, your purpose will best be served not in what you know and how you present it—though both are vital components for education—but in how devoted you are to the children you teach. If you become a doctor, your education and skill will be fully exercised only if your care and compassion are genuinely expressed.

The bottom line is, you'll find much greater fulfillment in serving humanity than could be found in any self-centered pursuit. The more you give your life away, the more purpose you'll discover in living.

Jesus knew this little secret. He said, "It is more blessed to give than to receive" (Acts 20:35).

Make this your highest aim: Live to give!

Rejection

Jesus said, "Here is a simple rule of thumb for behavior:
Ask yourself what you want people to do for you;
then grab the initiative and do it for them!"

LUKE 6:31 MSG

Jesus said, "Go at once into the streets and alleys of the town,
and bring in the poor, the crippled, the blind, and the lame."

LUKE 14:21 NCV

Jesus said, "To you who are ready for the truth, I say this:
Love your enemies. Let them bring out the best in you, not the
worst. When someone gives you a hard time, respond with the
energies of prayer for that person. If someone slaps you in the face,
stand there and take it. If someone grabs your shirt, giftwrap your
best coat and make a present of it. If someone takes unfair advantage
of you, use the occasion to practice the servant life.
No more tit-for-tat stuff. Live generously."

LUKE 6:27-30 MSG

Jesus said, "Those the Father has given me will come to me,
and I will never reject them."

JOHN 6:37 NLT

Jesus said, "The one who rejects you, rejects me.
And rejecting me is the same as rejecting God, who sent me."

LUKE 10:16 MSG

Heavenly Father:

Rejection is one of the most painful experiences there is. I have experienced it firsthand, so I know how deep the wounds can go, how destructive it can be, and how difficult it is to overcome.

I want to be the remedy for rejection in the lives of others. Give me the opportunity to extend Your love and acceptance to those who need it most. Bring to my attention people who feel excluded, left out, or alone. Give me ideas of how I can bring them into my group so that they will feel welcome and cherished for who You created them to be.

As for the cruel and selfish, give me an extra dose of compassion. Perhaps they have been warped by rejection. Use me to interject Your transforming love into their lives.

Amen.

THE GOLDEN RULE
FOR REJECTION

"I don't want to be your friend anymore."

"We don't want you on our team."

"You're not invited."

"Go away and leave us alone."

The terms of rejection you recognize from childhood are painful to recall. Some suffer more of these than others, but everyone knows an experience of painful exclusion. Rejection strikes at the very core of your being and sends ripples of heartache and insecurity through every dimension of life.

One productive way to deal with rejection is to make certain that no one ever suffers those feelings at your hands. How? By living the Golden Rule: Treat other people the way you want to be treated. It is amazing how therapeutic this can be. When you take a proactive approach to living a considerate and gracious lifestyle, the blessing ricochets back to you.

Try it for a week. Go out of your way to treat other people with genuine love and acceptance. Tell yourself that regardless of the disposition or behavior of those around you, you will not compromise your commitment to the Golden Rule.

Have mercy on rude people. Show compassion for mean ones. Love the unlovable. Include those who are usually left out. Make room for the ideas of others. Give credit to the efforts people make. And regardless of how busy you are, determine that you won't turn away from anyone intentionally.

Though you cannot control others' acceptance or rejection of you, you can take the initiative to accept and embrace other people. It is a sure remedy for the heartache of rejection.

My Precious Child:

Rejection warps people, skews their view of life, and prevents them from experiencing life to the full. It has the power to transform an innocent child into a cruel monster. On the other hand, My love transforms people too. It heals, restores, and makes all things new.

Jesus knows about rejection firsthand. But He endured it willingly because of love, a love that revolutionizes the lives of all who embrace it.

Thank you for your willingness to express My heart to the world. I will show you how you can love the unlovely and will give you strength to reach out to those whom others have rejected. I will give you unique opportunities to touch their lives in a way that no one ever has. Through you I will make Myself known to them and transform them through the power of My love.

Your loving Father

Relationships

Be humble and gentle. Be patient with each other, making allowance for each other's faults because of your love. Try always to be led along together by the Holy Spirit, and so be at peace with one another.

EPHESIANS 4:2-3 TLB

Concerning the pure brotherly love that there should be among God's people, I don't need to say very much, I'm sure! For God himself is teaching you to love one another.

1 THESSALONIANS 4:9 TLB

Jesus said, "Let me give you a new command: Love one another. In the same way I loved you, you love one another."

JOHN 13:34 MSG

You must get along with each other. You must learn to be considerate of one another, cultivating a life in common.

1 CORINTHIANS 1:10 MSG

Speak encouraging words to one another. Build up hope so you'll all be together in this, no one left out, no one left behind.

1 THESSALONIANS 5:11 MSG

BUILDING RELATIONSHIPS
THAT LAST

Strong relationships are of vital importance in every arena of life. Now that you've graduated, you're beginning many new relationships while your current ones are going through some changes. As you face these challenges, don't forget to seek God's advice. He has given you a whole list of ways that you can build strong relationships through practicing some "one anothers":

- Love one another. Love makes all the difference when it comes to keeping relationships strong. Love will come in different forms depending on the relationship, but it will always mean putting others first and thinking about what is best for them before you think about what is best for you.

- Encourage one another. Take the time to congratulate a coworker on a job well done or to send a note to a friend who is going through a rough time. Even little acts of encouragement can strengthen relationships.

- Live in harmony with one another. Make it your priority to resolve conflicts quickly and restore peace.

- Serve one another in love. Be willing to go out of your way to help someone who really needs it. You never know what even a little act of service can do in the life of a person who is in desperate need.

- Be kind and compassionate to one another. Put yourself in others' shoes and try to understand how they feel. Then do for them what you would want them to do for you in the same situation.

These are just a few of God's great relationship tips. If you'll use His advice as your guide, your life will be filled with strong and lasting relationships.

Responsibility

If God has given you leadership ability,
take the responsibility seriously.
ROMANS 12:8 NLT

Make a careful exploration of who you are and the work you have
been given, and then sink yourself into that. Don't be impressed
with yourself. Don't compare yourself with others.
Each of you must take responsibility for doing the creative best
you can with your own life.
GALATIANS 6:4-5 MSG

Servants, do what you're told by your earthly masters.
And don't just do the minimum that will get you by.
Do your best. Work from the heart for your real Master, for God.
COLOSSIANS 3:22-23 MSG

Be a responsible citizen and you'll get on just fine,
the government working to your advantage. But if you're breaking
the rules right and left, watch out. The police aren't there just
to be admired in their uniforms. God also has an interest in
keeping order, and he uses them to do it. That's why you must
live responsibly—not just to avoid punishment but also because it's
the right way to live. That's also why you pay taxes—so that an orderly
way of life can be maintained. Fulfill your obligations as a citizen.
Pay your taxes, pay your bills, respect your leaders.
ROMANS 13:3-7 MSG

THE BENEFITS OF BEING RESPONSIBLE

Now that you have graduated, you're probably hearing a lot about the importance of living a responsible life. You're probably also thinking that responsibility is not a very fun word. It conjures up thoughts of hard work and going to bed early and eating your vegetables. Being responsible can mean that you have to do some things that you don't really want to do, but it also brings with it many benefits that will actually make your life more enjoyable. God built the world to work that way.

When you are responsible in your job—doing your best work, showing up on time, and treating your coworkers with respect—you'll find that your work life is enjoyable and that promotions and raises will come your way sooner rather than later.

When you are responsible in your relationships—putting others ahead of yourself, making it a priority to spend time with loved ones, and treating everyone the way you would like to be treated—you'll gain true friends who will be there for you when you need them the most.

When you are responsible in taking care of your body— eating well, exercising, and getting enough sleep—you'll have the energy to do the things you want to do.

Responsibility isn't always fun. We all have to do things that we don't really like to do in order to keep our commitments and be responsible people. But when we do what it takes to meet our responsibilities, God will bless us with joy-filled lives.

Rest

Jesus said, "Come to me, all you that are weary and are carrying
heavy burdens, and I will give you rest. Take my yoke upon you,
and learn from me; for I am gentle and humble in heart,
and you will find rest for your souls."

MATTHEW 11:28-29 NRSV

By the seventh day God had finished the work he had been doing;
so on the seventh day he rested from all his work. And God blessed
the seventh day and made it holy, because on it he rested from all
the work of creating that he had done.

GENESIS 2:2-3

My soul finds rest in God alone;
my salvation comes from him.

PSALM 62:1

Anyone who enters God's rest also rests from his own work,
just as God did from his.

HEBREWS 4:10

God said, "Remember the Sabbath day, to keep it holy. Six days you
shall labor and do all your work, but the seventh day is the Sabbath
of the Lord your God. In it you shall do no work."

EXODUS 20:8-10 NKJV

Heavenly Father:

You know I have a lot on my plate. Everyone says I need to slow down and take a break, but how can I? I have so many responsibilities now—between my job, trying to keep up with my relationships, laundry, taking care of my car—the list goes on and on. I even have a hard time settling down to go to sleep at night. After I lie down, my mind keeps going about the things I have to do the next day. Then, in the morning, the routine starts all over again. It's a never-ending treadmill.

And there's another thing. I feel guilty if I take time out to rest. Even on my days off, I feel like I should be doing something productive. I guess I need Your help with this because I seem to have gotten out of balance.

Amen.

TAKE TIME TO REST

As a new graduate, you're probably discovering (if you haven't already) that life can be truly exhausting. There are so many demands on your time. Some days all you want to do is rest, but when you do, you feel guilty because of all the things that need to be done.

Why do you struggle with taking time out for rest? Do you fear that others will think you're lazy? Have you set your goals so high that you're afraid you'll fail if you don't keep up your breakneck pace? What do you think will happen to you, though, if you don't take time to rest?

God created us to work and be creative, but He also created us with a need to relax. He even took time out after creating the world to rest, just to show us how important it really is. And after He took a day off, He didn't just suggest that we do the same—He made it a commandment.

God knows that we need time for rest. We need built-in moments of quiet and peace to rejuvenate our bodies and our souls. We need time to reflect on what God is doing in our lives so that we won't lose perspective on what is really important.

So take time to rest at least once a week. Put aside all your task lists and spend time worshiping God, enjoying His creation, or even taking a long nap. Make rest a part of your schedule. When you obey God's command to rest, He will multiply your time and energy and help you get done what needs to be done.

My Precious Child:

Did you know that even I rest? I spent six days on Creation and on the seventh day, I kicked back to enjoy it all. Society doesn't honor the Sabbath anymore. In fact, most people probably don't even know what that is. But it is so important that I made it one of My commandments. A day of rest is vital to the health and well-being of all people. It gives spirit, soul, and body a chance to refuel. It is when you are still and quiet that I can speak to your heart and prepare you for the week to come.

Make sure you get enough sleep every night too. You'll find that by taking care of yourself with proper rest, you will be sharper and more creative, and you'll have more energy to tackle your busy life.

Your loving Father

Seeking God

You will call upon Me and go and pray to Me, and I will listen to you. And you will seek Me and find Me, when you search for Me with all your heart. I will be found by you, says the Lord.

JEREMIAH 29:12-14 NKJV

All who seek the Lord shall find him and shall praise his name.

PSALM 22:26 TLB

The humble shall see their God at work for them. No wonder they will be so glad! All who seek for God shall live in joy.

PSALM 69:32 TLB

Seek the Lord while you can find him.
Call upon him now while he is near.

ISAIAH 55:6 TLB

Jesus said, "Ask, and it will be given you; seek, and you will find; knock, and it will be opened to you. For every one who asks receives, and he who seeks finds, and to him who knocks it will be opened."

MATTHEW 7:7-8 RSV

Those who know your name put their trust in you,
for you, O LORD, have not forsaken those who seek you.

PSALM 9:10 NRSV

HE WILL BE FOUND

Have you ever wasted fifteen minutes looking all over the house for your keys, only to discover that they were hanging on the key hook beside the door, just where they were supposed to be? Or maybe you searched and searched for a roll of tape in your junk drawer and couldn't find it, but when you asked someone to help you, they found it in the drawer, right in front of your nose. Searching for something that was there to be found the whole time is frustrating.

As you start a new and unknown future after graduation, do you feel like you're searching for God and just can't seem to find Him? The good news is that, unlike your keys or that roll of tape, God wants to be found and will reveal Himself to you when you truly seek Him.

So how do you seek God? First of all, just like finding your keys on their hook, look for God in the places that you would normally expect Him to be. Read the Bible. Find a church and attend regularly. Take time to pray and listen for God's voice.

Second, ask someone else who seems to have found God to help you find Him as well. It may be, like that roll of tape, that He has been right in front of you all along, but you just need help to see Him.

When you sincerely seek God, He will never fail to come to you and open your eyes so that He can be found. So keep up your search. God promises to reveal Himself to you when you do.

Service

Never be lazy in your work but serve the Lord enthusiastically.
ROMANS 12:11 TLB

Jesus said, "Whoever wishes to become great among you
shall be your servant."
MATTHEW 20:26 NASB

Serve the Lord with gladness!
PSALM 100:2 RSV

Train yourself to serve God. Training your body helps you in some
ways, but serving God helps you in every way by bringing you
blessings in this life and in the future life, too.
1 TIMOTHY 4:7-8 NCV

Jesus said, "Your attitude must be like my own, for I,
the Messiah, did not come to be served, but to serve,
and to give my life as a ransom for many."
MATTHEW 20:28 TLB

Jesus said, "The one who serves you best will be your leader.
Out in the world the master sits at the table and is served by
his servants. But not here! For I am your servant."
LUKE 22:26-27 TLB

THE UNIVERSAL BLESSING
OF SERVICE

Service to others, especially those in need, is a universal value. People from all cultures and religions agree that helping out your fellow human beings is good and worthwhile because God created us to need other people. From the very beginning of time, God said that it wasn't good for people to be alone—that we need each other.

When you serve others with your special strengths, you are fulfilling God's purpose for the human race. Through acts of service, people receive what they are lacking and in turn gain the strength to serve others themselves.

When you help an elderly lady with household tasks that she is physically unable to do, you are using your strength to meet her need. In turn, she can use the wisdom that life has brought her to encourage you and give you sound advice.

When you give canned goods to a food pantry, you're using the provision that God has given you to provide for someone else. In turn, a single mother can feed her children and give them the strength they need to get an education and have a better life.

As a new graduate with many new responsibilities, you may find it hard to fit service into your schedule, but it will be worth the effort. The amazing thing about serving is that you always find yourself blessed as well.

We all need each other for strength and encouragement. God made the world to work that way. Every act of service, no matter how small, has an impact on someone's life. When you make service a priority, God will use you to change your world.

Spiritual Growth

We are bound to give thanks to God always for you . . .
because your faith is growing abundantly, and the love of every one
of you for one another is increasing.

2 THESSALONIANS 1:3 RSV

As newborn babes, desire the pure milk of the word,
that you may grow thereby.

1 PETER 2:2 NKJV

Jesus said, "What is the seed that fell on the good ground?
That seed is like the person who hears the teaching and
understands it. That person grows and produces fruit."

MATTHEW 13:23 NCV

We must become like a mature person, growing until we become
like Christ and have his perfection. . . . Speaking the truth with
love, we will grow up in every way into Christ, who is the head.

EPHESIANS 4:13,15 NCV

We pray that you will also have great wisdom and understanding in
spiritual things so that you will live the kind of life that honors and
pleases the Lord in every way. You will produce fruit in every good
work and grow in the knowledge of God.

COLOSSIANS 1:9-10 NCV

Heavenly Father:

I may have finished school, but there's still so much that I don't know. I'm excited about what I'm learning about You, but it can be overwhelming when I look at how big the Bible is. How will I ever learn all that is in it? Where do I begin?

And there's another thing I have a question about. I hear people talk about hearing Your voice, but I don't understand that. Do they really? And how do they know it's You? That would be awesome to hear You talking directly to me.

I am so hungry to learn about spiritual things, but I need some guidance. Lead me to mature believers who can mentor me and show me the ropes. I know that the only way I can fulfill my destiny is to grow up spiritually and do things Your way.

Amen.

GROWING UP IN GOD

Being a baby is great. All your needs are met, and you have no responsibilities. Your only job is to play and grow. Yes, life as a baby is pretty good.

But you can't stay a baby forever—and honestly, who would want to? While babyhood has its perks, it is also pretty limiting. You can't eat solid food or pick out your own clothes. Communicating with others is frustrating since you can't talk. And you have to be carried everywhere because you haven't learned the fine art of walking!

These same principles also apply to your spiritual growth. When you first believe in Jesus, you are a baby spiritually—and that's okay. Everyone has to start somewhere. Spiritual child-hood is the time to learn the basics about faith, love, and obeying God. It's the time to be nurtured by older Christians. At this stage your biggest responsibility should be growing and getting to know your Heavenly Father.

Once you have taken time to learn and grow, then you are ready to take on the responsibilities and receive the privileges of a more mature believer. Your Father wants you to take your first steps in ministry and try out using your gifts for Him. He also wants to use you to help other baby Christians learn. And the more you grow in your walk with God, the more blessings He will bring to your life.

Whether you are just becoming a believer or you are a mature believer who has walked with God for years, there is always room for growth. Take the hand of your Father and let Him lead you into a deeper walk with Him every day.

My Precious Child:

I created everything to grow. Look at nature and you'll see what I mean—not to mention your very own body. You know about physical growth firsthand.

Spiritual growth takes place in much the same way. Given the right combination of elements, any believer can grow to become a mighty person of faith.

Find a version of the Bible that you can understand, and read it every day. It will familiarize you with the way I talk so you will more easily recognize My voice when I speak to Your heart. Attending a church where you feel at home and hanging out with other believers will help you grow too. Then talk to Me every day. I'll lead you as you walk down My path, and before long, you will find yourself growing into the person I've destined you to be.

Your loving Father

Strength

[The Lord] said to me, "My grace is sufficient for you, for my power is made perfect in weakness." Therefore I will boast all the more gladly about my weaknesses, so that Christ's power may rest on me. That is why, for Christ's sake, I delight in weaknesses. . . . For when I am weak, then I am strong.

2 CORINTHIANS 12:9-10

I pray that from his glorious, unlimited resources he will give you mighty inner strength through his Holy Spirit.

EPHESIANS 3:16 NLT

May our Lord Jesus Christ and God our Father, who loved us and in his special favor gave us everlasting comfort and good hope, comfort your hearts and give you strength in every good thing you do and say.

2 THESSALONIANS 2:16-17 NLT

Those who hope in the LORD
will renew their strength.
They will soar on wings like eagles;
they will run and not grow weary,
they will walk and not be faint.

ISAIAH 40:31

A LIMITLESS SOURCE
OF STRENGTH

You're frantically working on a huge project at work. You spend every waking moment trying to finish. After a week at this pace, you're still swamped—plus you're exhausted and burned out. You finally sheepishly admit to your boss that you need help. He immediately asks two of your coworkers to pitch in, and together you finish the project with time to spare. You wonder why you didn't just ask for help in the first place!

How many times have you pushed yourself to the breaking point before you admitted that you needed help? In an effort to prove yourself in the "real world," you'll probably find it tempting to rely on your own strength.

The problem with trusting in your own strength is that it is limited. Eventually you're going to run down and burn out. The good news is that God's strength has no limits and He offers it to you whenever you ask.

There will be times when you'll need to enlist the help of others, but God's strength is always available. He wants to come to you when you are at your weakest point and infuse you with divine assistance. In fact, He says that when you are at your weakest, that is when His strength can shine through you most powerfully. When you are willing to admit that you don't have what it takes to succeed without God's help, He rushes to your side with His abundant strength.

So the next time you find yourself facing a monumental task or an incredibly difficult situation, why not ask God for His strength right away? He will be faithful to provide you with all you need.

Stress

As pressure and stress bear down on me,
I find joy in your commands.

PSALM 119:143 NLT

Jesus said, "The seed cast in the weeds represents the ones who hear
the kingdom news but are overwhelmed with worries about all the
things they have to do and all the things they want to get. The stress
strangles what they heard, and nothing comes of it. But the seed
planted in the good earth represents those who hear the Word,
embrace it, and produce a harvest beyond their wildest dreams."

MARK 4:18-20 MSG

Do not worry about anything, but pray and ask God for
everything you need, always giving thanks. And God's peace,
which is so great we cannot understand it, will keep your hearts
and minds in Christ Jesus.

PHILIPPIANS 4:6-7 NCV

I am guiding you in the way of wisdom,
and I am leading you on the right path.
Nothing will hold you back;
you will not be overwhelmed.

PROVERBS 4:11-12 NCV

DIVINE STRESS RELIEF

What is stressing you out now that you are out of school? Is it your new job? Is it a relationship that you feel should be further along than it is? Is it your bank account? Maybe it is all of the above!

Numerous books have been written on how to eliminate stress from your life. Some suggest reprioritizing your time. Others tell you to exercise and make healthier diet choices. Still others tell you to spend more time taking care of yourself.

While all of these suggestions have some merit, there is one book that truly has some powerful antidotes to stress. Through the Bible, God has given us lots of guidance about combating stress and living peace-filled lives:

- When you're stressed about money and bills, remember that God knows what you need before you even ask. You can always trust Him to take care of you and provide for you.
- When people put you down for doing the right thing, remember that God will reward you and bless you when you stand firm for Him.
- When you feel overwhelmed and exhausted, God promises you rest. He wants to give you the strength to persevere through hard times.
- When you are confused and need direction, God says that all you need to do is ask for His guidance, and He will show you the way and give you incredible peace at the same time.

The Bible is full of stress-relieving promises. Take some time each day to let them sink into your soul, and you'll find your stress level getting lower and your sense of peace expanding!

Success

In everything you do, put God first, and he will direct you
and crown your efforts with success.

PROVERBS 3:6 TLB

Whoever tries to live right and be loyal
finds life, success, and honor.

PROVERBS 21:21 NCV

Depend on the LORD in whatever you do,
and your plans will succeed.

PROVERBS 16:3 NCV

Wisdom has the advantage of giving success.

ECCLESIASTES 10:10 NASB

David had success in all his undertakings;
for the LORD was with him.

1 SAMUEL 18:14 RSV

Lord our God, treat us well.
Give us success in what we do;
yes, give us success in what we do.

PSALM 90:17 NCV

Heavenly Father:

Everyone wants to be a success in life, including me, but there seem to be different standards of what that really means. When I see people driving luxury cars, wearing designer clothes, and living in the finest homes, they look like the picture of success. And that's what most people would say. But there has to be more to it than that—even a criminal can look good!

Sure I want to enjoy that kind of success, but more than anything I want to be a success in Your eyes. I want to live my life on purpose—the purpose that You created me for. I want to enjoy eternal rewards, not just earthly ones.

Help me to accept each opportunity You give me to do life Your way so that my success brings honor to You.

Amen.

TRUE SUCCESS

As a new graduate you are probably thinking a lot about success. You want to live a successful life and have a successful career. But what is true success? How should you define it? How can you know when you've achieved it?

You are bombarded every day with messages about being successful. Commercials tell you that being successful means having a new car, a big house, and the hippest clothes. At work you get the sense that success means working long hours, getting promotions, and making more money. And your friends seem to think that success means having fun and living life your own way.

While having nice things, a good job, and fun leisure time are all good things, they aren't what God uses as His measure of success. To be truly successful in His eyes is to live your life fulfilling the purpose He has designed for you, loving Him, and loving others. When you pursue excellence in these areas, everything else will fall into place.

When you love God through obeying Him and love others by putting their interests above your own, you'll find that success will come to you in every arena of your life. As you strive to live for God in your work life, He will bless you with new opportunities and good working relationships. And when you truly love others by putting them first, you'll find that your relationships with family and friends will grow deeper and bring you a joy that is priceless.

So put aside all the other voices and follow God's plan for success. He will bless you in amazing ways when you seek to fulfill the purpose He has for you.

My Precious Child:

I don't measure success like most people do. It's not about what you can see on the outside, but what a person is inside that counts with Me. And the world goes about achieving their success in exactly the opposite way that I do. The world's way is to look out for number one, but to become great in My kingdom, you must put others first. Instead of stepping on people to get to the top, My way is to lay down your life for them and become the servant of all.

There's nothing wrong with enjoying the trappings of a prosperous life, but true success is found only through fulfilling the purpose for which I created You and doing it My way.

Your loving Father

Talent

Just as our bodies have many parts and each part has a
special function, so it is with Christ's body. We are all parts of his
one body, and each of us has different work to do. And since we are
all one body in Christ, we belong to each other, and each
of us needs all the others. God has given each of us the
ability to do certain things well.

ROMANS 12:4-6 NLT

There are different kinds of spiritual gifts, but it is the same
Holy Spirit who is the source of them all. There are different kinds
of service in the church, but it is the same Lord we are serving.
There are different ways God works in our lives, but it is the same
God who does the work through all of us. A spiritual gift is given to
each of us as a means of helping the entire church. . . . It is the one
and only Holy Spirit who distributes these gifts. He alone
decides which gift each person should have.

1 CORINTHIANS 12:4-7,11 NLT

Remember the LORD your God, for it is he who gives you
the ability to produce wealth.

DEUTERONOMY 8:18

Moses said, "Come, all of you who are skilled craftsmen having
special talents, and construct what God has commanded us."

EXODUS 35:10 TLB

RISK AND REWARDS

Jesus once told the story of a businessman who left three of his employees with various amounts of money to manage for him while he went on a trip. When the boss returned, he had his employees report on what they had done with the money. Two of the employees had invested and doubled the amounts they had been given. But the third man decided not to take the risk of investing and simply buried the money. The businessman gave high praise to the two who invested but expressed deep disappointment in the one who didn't even try. (See Matthew 25:14–30.)

So what does this story have to do with you as a graduate? God has given you certain gifts and talents. If you don't put them to use, they are going to be wasted. Stepping out in faith to follow God's purpose may involve some fear and uncertainty. You may feel like burying your talents and avoiding the hard work it takes to do what God has called you to do. But as you can see from Jesus' story, it was those who risked it all who were rewarded in the end.

Are you settling for an easy job instead of one that challenges you to use your abilities? Are you avoiding an opportunity to use your gifts in your church because it will take up too much of your free time? If so, you're missing out on seeing what God will do when you use your gifts for Him. So ask God today to give you the courage and passion to use the talents He has given you. The return on your investment will be greater than you can imagine.

Thoughts

Those who live following their sinful selves think only about things
that their sinful selves want. But those who live following the Spirit
are thinking about the things the Spirit wants them to do.
If people's thinking is controlled by the sinful self,
there is death. But if their thinking is controlled by the Spirit,
there is life and peace.

ROMANS 8:5-6 NCV

They delight in doing everything God wants them to, and day and
night are always meditating on his laws and thinking about ways to
follow him more closely. They are like trees along a river bank
bearing luscious fruit each season without fail. Their leaves shall
never wither, and all they do shall prosper.

PSALM 1:2-3 TLB

I am always thinking of the Lord; and because he is so near,
I never need to stumble or to fall.

PSALM 16:8 TLB

Whatever is true, whatever is honorable, whatever is just,
whatever is pure, whatever is pleasing, whatever is commendable,
if there is any excellence and if there is anything worthy of praise,
think about these things.

PHILIPPIANS 4:8 NRSV

THINK ABOUT IT

What occupies most of your thoughts now that you're a graduate? Maybe you spend a lot of time thinking about the future or about your finances as you try to make ends meet on your own. Or perhaps you're enjoying the fact that your studies are over, and you're letting your mind have a rest in front of the TV.

Did you know that what you think about plays a big part in who you are and what you do? The Bible has a lot to say about the importance of your thought life and how it can ultimately affect your behavior.

- What you think about the most indicates what is most important to you—the Bible calls it your treasure. What you treasure becomes your focus and priority in life. It makes sense, then, to be sure that the things you think about the most are worthy of being treasured.
- Your thoughts lead to actions. What may seem like an innocent bit of fantasizing can easily turn into actions that you may regret later, if you let it continue to fill your mind.
- Even if you never tell anyone what you are thinking, God knows your thoughts. The good news is that you can ask Him to help you root out the ones that aren't pleasing to Him; and He has given you a multitude of positive, uplifting, and productive things to focus on in the Bible.

Pay attention to what passes through your mind today. Ask yourself where the thoughts might lead and what God would think of them. He'll help you treasure the things that lead to life and joy if you ask for His help.

Time

Listen for God's voice in everything you do, everywhere you go;
he's the one who will keep you on track.
PROVERBS 3:6 MSG

See then that you walk circumspectly, not as fools but as wise,
redeeming the time, because the days are evil.
EPHESIANS 5:15-16 NKJV

I'm writing out clear directions to Wisdom Way,
I'm drawing a map to Righteous Road.
I don't want you ending up in blind alleys,
or wasting time making wrong turns.
PROVERBS 4:11-12 MSG

To every thing there is a season,
and a time to every purpose under the heaven.
ECCLESIASTES 3:1 KJV

Don't procrastinate—
there's no time to lose.
PROVERBS 6:4 MSG

Heavenly Father:

When I was younger, time seemed to pass so slowly, but now it seems to be going faster and faster. I remember being bored as a child with nothing to do. Now I'd give anything to be bored once in a while! Instead, there just aren't enough hours in the day.

Sometimes I feel that I need help, especially on my job, but I am afraid to ask. I think surely I should be able to do everything myself. I don't want to appear incompetent. Is that being prideful?

I need help to know how to budget my time more wisely. Help me see where I may be wasting time and how I can use it more efficiently. You have given me twenty-four hours each day. I want to get the most out of every single one.

Amen.

GOD'S TIME-MANAGEMENT TIPS

You've been running at full speed for so long, and now that graduation is over, it doesn't look like you'll be slowing down anytime soon. You're in the real world now, and once again you're finding that there don't seem to be enough hours in the day.

When you're feeling overwhelmed with all the responsibilities of a full life, God is right there by your side with some guidelines to help you manage your time:

- God says to devote your time to those things that are truly important. Take an honest look at how you spend your time for one whole week, and see if there are some activities that you can cut out to make room for more important priorities.

- Seek to please God first and people second. It's okay for you to say no sometimes. God doesn't want you to burn out trying to please all of the people all of the time. When you seek to please Him first, He'll give you discernment on what He wants you to do and when.

- God made us to need other people. Ask for help when you are overwhelmed. Two can always accomplish more than one.

- As strange as it may sound, an important key to managing your time is rest. God built a day of rest into each week to give you a chance to catch your breath and let Him restore your body, mind, and spirit.

Life is hectic. But if you'll follow God's time-management tips, He will help you accomplish all that is necessary. In turn you will experience the deep abiding sense of fulfillment of a life well lived.

My Precious Child:

Feeling overwhelmed and stressed is not part of My plan. I am the God of peace. Putting in a full day's work is a good thing, but working overtime every day and never having any downtime is actually counterproductive. Start your mornings with Me and make sure you have time to unwind each day. Next, invest in your significant relationships.

As for the remainder of your time, the answers you need are in your heart. The main thing is to follow peace. I don't use pressure or guilt to guide you.

Keep in mind, you are not compelled to say yes to every request made of you. It's hard to say no, but sometimes it is the right thing to do. Remember, you are here to make a difference. Make every minute count.

Your loving Father

Time Alone

At daybreak Jesus went out to a solitary place.

LUKE 4:42

After [Jesus] had dismissed the crowds,
he went up on the mountain by himself to pray.
When evening came, he was there alone.

MATTHEW 14:23 RSV

In the morning, rising up a great while before day, [Jesus] went out,
and departed into a solitary place, and there prayed.

MARK 1:35 KJV

The apostles gathered around Jesus and reported to him all they
had done and taught. Then, because so many people were coming
and going that they did not even have a chance to eat, he said to
them, "Come with me by yourselves to a quiet place and get some
rest." So they went away by themselves in a boat to a solitary place.

MARK 6:30-32

[The Lord] makes me lie down in green pastures,
he leads me beside quiet waters,
he restores my soul.

PSALM 23:2-3

IT'S OKAY TO BE ALONE

You've just graduated and your schedule is already packed full. You're excited about all the new opportunities available to you and you've thrown yourself wholeheartedly into your job, your developing relationships, and some enriching volunteer work. You love being involved in so many great things, yet sometimes you find yourself feeling exhausted and close to burnout. You know that doing your best and offering yourself in service to others is pleasing to God—but sometimes you'd just like to have some time alone. Is it wrong to want some solitude once in a while?

The truth is that spending time alone is not only okay, it is a practice that God encourages us to develop through the example of Jesus. On more than one occasion during His ministry on earth, Jesus left the crowds of sick and needy people that surrounded Him to take time to be alone. He knew that if He was to continue to fulfill His mission, He had to build times of solitude and prayer into His busy schedule.

So follow Jesus' example and make time to be alone with God. Take a walk in the woods and enjoy the beauty around you. Sit on a park bench and watch kids play while you chat with God. Cuddle up in your favorite chair with your Bible and some coffee, and let God speak to you through His Word. Through time alone with your Heavenly Father, you'll find new energy and inspiration for the great mission He has given you.

Trust

The works of his hands are faithful and just;
all his precepts are trustworthy.

PSALM 111:7 RSV

The Lord said to me, "You have seen correctly,
because I am watching to make sure my words come true."

JEREMIAH 1:12 NCV

All you need to remember is that God will never let you down;
he'll never let you be pushed past your limit; he'll always be there
to help you come through it.

1 CORINTHIANS 10:13 MSG

Since God assured us, "I'll never let you down,
never walk off and leave you," we can boldly quote,
God is there, ready to help; I'm fearless no matter what.
Who or what can get to me?

HEBREWS 13:5-6 MSG

The statutes you have laid down are righteous;
they are fully trustworthy.

PSALM 119:138

YOU CAN TRUST HIM

Trust is a vital component of any strong relationship. But trust is fragile—it can be easily broken. Perhaps that is why fully trusting God is so difficult. When someone you love breaks your trust, it can make it hard to believe that God won't let you down as well.

When you're struggling to trust God, especially now in this uncertain time after graduation, turn to His Word. It is filled with stories of people who chose to trust God and found that He never broke a promise.

Abraham was an elderly man with an elderly wife, yet God promised him that he would have a son and that through that child, Abraham would become the father of God's people. Abraham trusted God, and through his son Isaac came the entire nation of Israel.

David was just a teenager when he fought and killed a nine-foot-tall armored giant with only a slingshot. Because he trusted in God to win the battle, David saved his people and went on to become their king.

When Mary was told that she would become pregnant with the very Son of God, she trusted God for what seemed impossible. Through God's work in her, the whole world has been blessed with a Savior.

These are just a few of the many accounts of people who were rewarded for their trust in God. You may even find that people in your life have their own incredible stories about the benefits of trusting God. No matter who has let you down, God wants to prove to you that He is worthy of your trust. Open your heart and let Him reassure you of His promises.

Truth

Jesus said, "As it is written in the Scriptures,
'They shall all be taught of God.' Those the Father speaks to,
who learn the truth from him, will be attracted to me."

JOHN 6:45 TLB

Jesus said, "You will know the truth,
and the truth will make you free."

JOHN 8:32 NASB

Jesus said, "I am the way, the truth, and the life.
No one can come to the Father except through me."

JOHN 14:6 NLT

The Lord's promise is sure. He speaks no careless word;
all he says is purest truth, like silver seven times refined.

PSALM 12:6 TLB

A wise person is hungry for truth,
while the fool feeds on trash.

PROVERBS 15:14 NLT

Truth stands the test of time.

PROVERBS 12:19 NLT

Heavenly Father:

What is the truth? And how will I know when I find it? I hear about relative truth and absolute truth. Which is right? Are things really as black-and-white as some say? Does the truth vary from person to person? Does it change over time? It's all quite confusing, but I need to know if I am going to build a successful life on a firm foundation.

I think it used to be easier to tell right from wrong, but these days one person may claim that something is okay, while another claims the very same thing is wrong. I want to know what You consider to be the truth and how it applies to my life. Only You are wise enough to hold the answers, and You are the only one I trust to be my guide.

Amen.

THE QUESTION OF TRUTH

What is truth? As a graduate you have probably already been in a few discussions (or at least sat through a few lectures) concerning this question. This is the biggest question of the human race, and many have tried to answer it throughout the centuries.

Some people say that we all have to search for our own personal truth. Others say that truth is a deep and hidden mystery and even if we spend our whole lives searching, we will never really find it. And some people say that the question of truth doesn't really matter because our world is run by chance and accident.

None of these answers are very satisfying. That's why people keep asking the question and searching. We all know deep down that finding truth is important and that somewhere it is out there to be found.

Two thousand years ago, a man named Jesus made some bold statements about the nature of truth. He said that if you followed His teachings you would know the truth and the truth would make you free. He said that the Word of God was truth. He said that He had been born to testify to the truth and that anyone who believed Him was also on the side of truth. He pronounced that He, in fact, was the truth.

Jesus is the answer to your search for truth. He came into this world to show us all what truth really is. We don't need to keep searching and wondering, because Jesus has revealed the truth to us. All we have to do is believe in Him.

My Precious Child:

I can understand why you are confused, but it's not as complicated as it seems. To make sure that there is no mistaking the truth, I have provided My Word. It is filled with everything you need to know to build a successful life on a rock-solid foundation. Its wisdom never changes, and it is powerful enough to transform circumstances and people when applied.

I have also given My Son Jesus who is the truth. One of the reasons I sent Him to earth was to be a living example of what truth in action looks like. When you are faced with situations and are not sure how to respond, try asking yourself, What would Jesus do? and the answer will usually become obvious.

Stay full of My Word and look to Jesus as your example, and you can't go wrong. It's the truth!

Your loving Father

Uncertainty

The wisdom from above is . . . without uncertainty.
JAMES 3:17 RSV

Jehoshaphat said, "We don't know what to do,
so we look to you [Lord] for help."
2 CHRONICLES 20:12 NCV

Lead me in the right path, O LORD. . . .
Tell me clearly what to do,
and show me which way to turn.
PSALM 5:8 NLT

Some people say, "Ask the mediums and fortune-tellers . . .
what to do." But I tell you that people should ask their God for
help. Why should people who are still alive ask something from the
dead? You should follow the teachings and the agreement with the
LORD. The mediums and fortune-tellers do not speak the word of
the LORD, so their words are worth nothing.
ISAIAH 8:19-20 NCV

They know exactly what to do and when to do it.
Their God is their teacher.
ISAIAH 28:26 MSG

THE GOODNESS IN UNCERTAINTY

Uncertainty is a big part of your life as a new graduate. Maybe you've sent out ten résumés, but you still don't have a job. Or you're looking for an apartment and nothing is available—where are you going to live?

Living in a state of uncertainty is uncomfortable, yet uncertainty can be a good thing. When you are facing the unknown, you are more likely to seek God's guidance. Uncertainty helps you realize that God is in control. While it may not be fun, living through an uncertain time helps you grow in your relationship with God.

In the Bible you can read about many people who learned to trust God through times of uncertainty. David had to trust God for protection as he ran for his life from King Saul who was trying to murder him. God kept David safe, and he went on to write a whole book of poetry about his trustworthy God.

Esther was a young Jewish woman married to a foreign king when she was informed of a plot to exterminate her people. She boldly approached her powerful husband with a plea to save the Jewish nation, even though going into his throne room without being asked could have resulted in her death. But she chose to trust God, no matter what the outcome. God proved faithful once again, and the Jews were saved from destruction.

As you face the stress that comes with the unknown, remember that God may be using this time to show you His love and concern for you in a new way. Let uncertainty drive you to pray and seek God through His Word and you, too, will find Him faithful.

Unselfishness

Jesus said to the disciples, "If any of you wants to be my follower, you must put aside your selfish ambition, shoulder your cross, and follow me."

MATTHEW 16:24 NLT

Let all men know and perceive and recognize your unselfishness (your considerateness, your forbearing spirit).

PHILIPPIANS 4:5 AMP

Do nothing from selfishness or conceit, but in humility count others better than yourselves. Let each of you look not only to his own interests, but also to the interests of others.

PHILIPPIANS 2:3-4 RSV

Where jealousy and selfish ambition exist, there is disorder and every evil thing. But the wisdom from above is first pure, then peaceable, gentle, reasonable, full of mercy and good fruits.

JAMES 3:16-17 NASB

Those who belong to Christ Jesus have crucified their own sinful selves. They have given up their old selfish feelings and the evil things they wanted to do.

GALATIANS 5:24 NCV

CHOOSING HOW TO LIVE

Our culture is full of messages about getting all you can get out of life, looking out for number one, and not letting anything or anyone stand in the way of your goals. On the other hand, God calls you to give all you can, to look out for others ahead of yourself, and to put your goals aside so that you can fulfill His purposes.

So which message is true? As you step out into the adult world and begin to make your own way after graduation, you're going to have to choose which way you want to live.

- When you selfishly put yourself first, ignoring the needs of others, you harden the hearts of those around you, as well as your own. But when you set your interests aside to put someone else's needs first, hearts are softened, and meaningful relationships are forged.
- When you make it your goal to get as much "stuff" as you can, you'll find that you are only left wanting more. But when you share even the little you have with others, you both receive blessing.
- When you selfishly hold on to your pride and refuse to seek help when you need it, you'll only end up alone and overwhelmed. But when you let go of pride and admit your needs, you'll find help and discover the joy of working as a team.

Which way do you want to live your life? Will you grab all you can for yourself and step on anyone who gets in your way? Or will you seek to live a life that will bring both you and your Heavenly Father great joy? The choice is yours.

Wisdom

There's nothing better than being wise. . . .
Wisdom puts light in the eyes.

ECCLESIASTES 8:1 MSG

Wisdom will make your life pleasant
and will bring you peace.
As a tree produces fruit, wisdom gives life to those who use it,
and everyone who uses it will be happy.

PROVERBS 3:17-18 NCV

To get wisdom is to love oneself;
to keep understanding is to prosper.

PROVERBS 19:8 NRSV

Fools think their own way is right,
but the wise listen to advice.

PROVERBS 12:15 NRSV

Wisdom is the principal thing. . . .
Exalt her, and she will promote you;
She will bring you honor, when you embrace her.

PROVERBS 4:7-8 NKJV

Heavenly Father:

I have gained a lot of knowledge through all my years in school; but as far as learning to live in the real world, well—I'm going to need Your wisdom for that.

I'm faced with a lot of decisions right now, and I don't want to make mistakes that could cost me time and money. You already know my future even better than I know my past, and I ask You to guide my steps day by day. Fill my mind with Your insight, and if I start to veer off the road, tug at my heart to get me back on course.

I know that Your Word is the ultimate source of wisdom, and I ask You to guide me as I look to it for answers. Use it to light my way.

Amen.

FINDING TRUE WISDOM

As you begin the new challenges of life as a graduate, you are quickly discovering your need for wisdom. You're facing big decisions and many new responsibilities. So where do you find the wisdom you need for this new chapter in your life?

Searching for wisdom is important and vital to your growth, but you need to be careful about where you conduct your search. When you're dealing with the big, deep issues of adulthood, it's easy to think that the wisdom you need is "out there" somewhere and that the simple wisdom you've grown up with just doesn't apply. The truth is, though, that much of the wisdom that the world offers isn't really wise at all. When it comes to finding true wisdom for your life's journey, you can't do any better than the simple, straightforward words of God.

When you have a big decision to make, God says to pray and ask for His guidance, seek out advice from wise people in your life, and make your decision based not just on your needs but on the interests of others as well.

When you're faced with a difficult new responsibility, God, again, says, pray—ask for His help and provision. Don't go it alone; ask for help from others. Then do your best to fulfill your responsibility in a way that would make God proud.

Finding true wisdom is a lifelong quest, but it doesn't have to be a mysterious journey. God hasn't hidden His wisdom from you—He's spelled it out in black-and-white in His Word. Follow His simple yet profound wisdom, and you'll never go wrong.

My Precious Child:

I am so glad You have asked for My wisdom. I have an endless supply of it, available whenever and wherever you need it. All of the Bible is a book of wisdom, but Proverbs is specifically dedicated to wise principles. There are thirty-one chapters, so read one each day to receive your "minimum daily requirement."

Wisdom is a many-faceted jewel and you can never exhaust its riches. Mine it often for nuggets guaranteed to give you a happy, long, and prosperous life. Be on the lookout for wise people who have walked the road you are traveling. I'll make sure just the right ones cross your path to give you a word in season when you need it.

I have awesome plans for you and am eager to get them underway.

Your loving Father

Work

Easy come, easy go,
but steady diligence pays off.

PROVERBS 13:11 MSG

When you eat the labor of your hands,
You shall be happy, and it shall be well with you.

PSALM 128:2 NKJV

Do your work with enthusiasm. Work as if you were serving the
Lord, not as if you were serving only men and women.

EPHESIANS 6:7 NCV

My life is worth nothing unless I use it for doing
the work assigned me by the Lord Jesus.

ACTS 20:24 NLT

In all the work you are doing, work the best you can. Work as if you
were doing it for the Lord, not for people. Remember that you will
receive your reward from the Lord, which he promised to his
people. You are serving the Lord Christ.

COLOSSIANS 3:23-24 NCV

The plans of the diligent lead surely to abundance.

PROVERBS 21:5 NRSV